William H. Jennings, Ph D

---

731 Dorset Road
Allentown, PA 18104
610-530-1695
email: franbill@enter.net

STORMS OVER GENESIS

STORMS
OVER
GENESIS

BIBLICAL BATTLEGROUND
IN AMERICA'S WARS OF RELIGION

WILLIAM H. JENNINGS

Fortress Press
MINNEAPOLIS

STORMS OVER GENESIS
BIBLICAL BATTLEGROUND
IN AMERICA'S WARS OF RELIGION

Cover images: July 1925: Clarence Darrow, defense lawyer, questioning William Jennings Bryan, director of the prosecution, about the Bible during the Scopes "Monkey Trial," Dayton, Tennessee. Photo © Hulton Archive / Getty Images (top). Photo © Mike Bentley / iStockphoto.com (bottom).
Cover design: Laurie Ingram
Book design: Ann Delgehausen, Trio Bookworks

Library of Congress Cataloging-in-Publication Data

Jennings, William H.
  Storms over Genesis : biblical battleground in America's wars of religion / William H. Jennings.
      p. cm.
Includes bibliographical references and index.
ISBN 13: 9780800662110 (alk. paper)

1. Bible. O.T. Genesis I–III—Criticism, interpretation, etc. 2. Creation.
3. Cosmogony. 4. Creationism. 5. United States—Church history.
  BS651 .J46 2007
                                             222/.110609 22

To my two beloved daughters,
Cathy and Sherry

CONTENTS

PREFACE

NO WORDS ever recorded have had more influence upon human affairs in more diverse ways than the words of the first three chapters of Genesis. The two creation stories in these chapters serve as the basis for Christian, Jewish, and Muslim views of the world and for how humans relate to the creator of that world. From a secular perspective, they have had a major influence upon the development of science and upon the justifications for capitalist economic systems. They serve as a background for both religious and secular understandings of how men and women relate to each other, as well as relationships within a family. And they are cited in debates about homosexuality.

Important things are never simple, and inevitably they generate controversy. This is certainly true of the opening chapters of Genesis, which are cited often in some of the stormiest debates of our time. Our study will be an analysis of the use of Genesis in three of these controversies. We note them here, with a sample question from each to illustrate what our study will be addressing.

Feminists. Genesis describes woman as created to be man's helper and then goes on to say she is the first to disobey God, thus introducing sin into the world. Is this not the beginning of many of the problems women face, as a woman still today is widely thought to be the weaker one who must take her husband's name and follow him?

Environmentalists. Genesis gives humans a special place in the created order, with humans alone created "in the image of God" and humans alone being told "to have dominion" over the rest of creation. Is this not the beginning of the idea that the earth belongs to us godlike humans and may be used any way that we desire, an idea that leads to the abuses so common in human relations with the natural world?

Creationists. Genesis describes in clear language how the world came into existence in a span of six days and tells us that God intended humans to be central in this creation. This is God's revelation, many say. If it disagrees with the theory of Darwin and other evolutionists, must not people of faith stand firm in supporting the biblical account?

The interpretations of Genesis from these three perspectives will be considered in some detail, along with views of those who say they get it all wrong and do not understand Genesis correctly. Our study will require focused Bible study, with attention to what the two stories in Genesis actually say and to insights from scholars of the Hebrew Bible.

Underlying the debates is also a larger issue. *Do the creation stories still have standing?* Many in the secular and scientific communities reject the stories as useless relics from earlier times. Even for some in Judaism and Christianity, the stories have lost their importance with the coming of new methods of understanding the Bible and with the inroads of modern science. Critics have mounted sustained attacks and, a major blow, some have said there are better creation stories—stories that come from cultures more in tune with the natural world or stories drawing from women's experiences or molded by science.

The stories do reflect the world from which they came and are based on an outdated cosmology. They proclaim an "anthropomorphic, one-planet deity"[1] who seems in some ways different from the God whom many worship today. At one time the stories may have encouraged believers to stand in awe before the greatness of creation, but awe today is more likely to come from an encounter with pictures from the Hubble telescope or from descriptions by astrophysicists of the vast expanses of the universe. Indeed, for a heartfelt response to the magnificent universe, some Jews and Christians turn to the Psalms and not to Genesis.

Yet on this bumpy road, the creation stories still have considerable meaning for many. The focus of the stories is on the human and on how humans relate to the created world and its creator. Yes, we *may* argue over whether the stories focus too much on the human, and we *must* admit that they have been read as focusing too much on male humans. But when balanced with new insights—a need for symbiosis between humans and the natural world, a reformulated appreciation of the female, and a willing acceptance of the insights of today's science—this human drama may take on new life and provide continuing insights for those who wrestle with it.

The stories have been with us for over two and a half millennia. Over and over they have been recited and studied, and that process continues. Each age brings new concerns, as the twenty-first century is now doing, and the stories have entered into dialogue with that age. They are survivors and will be around centuries from now. These are amazing stories.

Anyone who studies them carefully is likely to end up with a deep respect.

Most of this study will focus on Christianity in America, for that is where the debates are most intense and interesting. Jewish views will also become part of the discussions at times. Attention will not be paid to Islam, although the Western Abrahamic tradition includes Islam along with Judaism and Christianity. Islam recognizes Genesis as its own, and there are references to the creation and to Adam and Eve in the Qur'an. But Islam has only recently entered the American religious landscape, and Muslims have yet to become an integrated part of the rumble-tumble scene of open debate that characterizes so much of American religion. Muslim authors have produced books and articles relating to our topics, but they are largely apologetic, arguing that the all-wise Quran has much to contribute; they do not have the self-criticism that is the focus of our study, so Islam will not be dealt with in these pages.

Our focus will be upon how Christians and Jews who call for changes in the religion that they follow face off verbally against those who take a more defensive and traditional stand. In a way each opposing camp thinks of its stand as a struggle for the heart of the religion, and they indeed are correct, for the degree to which change is rejected or accepted will affect the religions into the future. There are certainly many outside these religions who are critical, often radically so, but these also will not be part of our study. The views and debates considered are from *within* Christianity and Judaism.

Before beginning, it is appropriate for an author to tell something about himself and his reasons for writing. I taught at the college level for a number of years, and the topics addressed in this study often came into my teaching. I often found them to be doorways into a number of pivotal issues in American religion today—such as the nature of God, the authority of scripture, the struggle to be faithful to a historic faith in the light of modern challenges—and these issues will be explored in these pages.

I grew up in North Carolina, in a culture where Bible reading and prayer were as common in public schools as racial segregation. In effect I went to Protestant parochial schools disguised as public schools, an educational setup similar to what some would like to restore by the inclusion of creationist views into the curriculum. Some friends and family have always been fundamentalists and part of a conservative Protestant culture that I know well. William Jennings Bryan of the Scopes trial is a distant relative.

My graduate education at a Lutheran seminary and at Yale University was steeped in neoorthodoxy and in patriarchal Christianity, and earlier I thought of God as "wholly other." When I married a half century ago, educated women became nurses or teachers or secretaries and were missing from the academic fields that I chose. There clearly has been a shaking of my foundations at many points, and I have come to recognize the need for major changes in much of the Christianity that I have known.

My studies have led me to compare the creation myths of many religious traditions, and I appreciate especially the outlooks of Buddhists and of the American Indians. I have come to think of the creation stories in Genesis as part of a common human quest for origins. In the field of comparative religion, these stories of origin are called myths, and that term is appropriate for the Genesis stories. In biblical studies and in Judaism and Christianity, "creation story" rather than "myth" is the more common term, so we will be speaking of creation stories.

Finally, I wish to express special thanks to Darrell Jodock and Nelvin Vos, plus Donald and Beverly Hensler, great friends who read all or parts of the manuscript and offered most helpful advice. Thanks also to Kelly Cannon of the Muhlenberg College library for excellent research help. And highest appreciation must go to my wife, Frankie, who read the entire manuscript and gave invaluable support throughout the writing process.

TRANSLATIONS USED IN THIS STUDY
(See appendix A for notes on translations)

THE PRIMARY TRANSLATION

NRSV   *The New Revised Standard Version Bible with Apocrypha* (New York: Oxford University Press, 1991). Copyright 1989 by the Division of Christian Education of the National Council of Churches in the United States of America.

OTHER TRANSLATIONS CITED

KJ   *The Holy Bible* ("authorized" by King James, 1611; New York: Thomas Nelson and Sons, n. d.

RSV   *The Holy Bible, Revised Standard Version* (New York: Thomas Nelson and Sons, 1952)

NAB   *The New American Bible* (Washington, D.C.: Confraternity of Christian Doctrine, 1970). Approved by the United States Conference of Catholic Bishops.

NIV   *The Holy Bible, New International Version*
            (Grand Rapids: Zondervan, 1984). First
            published in 1978. The best-selling English
            translation.

TNIV   *The Holy Bible, Today's New International*
            Version (Grand Rapids: Zondervan, 2005). The
            NIV with inclusive language.

TANAKH   *TANAKH: The Holy Scriptures* (New York:
            Jewish Publication Society, 1999)

GENESIS 1–3
(New Revised Standard Version)

GENESIS 1

In the beginning when God created the heavens and the earth, [2]the earth was a formless void and darkness covered the face of the deep, while a wind from God swept over the face of the waters. [3]Then God said, "Let there be light"; and there was light. [4]And God saw that the light was good; and God separated the light from the darkness. [5]God called the light Day, and the darkness he called Night. And there was evening and there was morning, the first day.

[6]And God said, "Let there be a dome in the midst of the waters, and let it separate the waters from the waters." [7]So God made the dome and separated the waters that were under the dome from the waters that were above the dome. And it was so. [8]God called the dome Sky. And there was evening and there was morning, the second day.

[9]And God said, "Let the waters under the sky be gathered together into one place, and let the dry land appear." And it was so. [10]God called the dry land Earth, and the waters that were gathered together he called Seas. And God saw that it

was good. [11]Then God said, "Let the earth put forth vegetation: plants yielding seed, and fruit trees of every kind on earth that bear fruit with the seed in it." And it was so. [12]The earth brought forth vegetation: plants yielding seed of every kind, and trees of every kind bearing fruit with the seed in it. And God saw that it was good. [13]And there was evening and there was morning, the third day.

[14]And God said, "Let there be lights in the dome of the sky to separate the day from the night; and let them be for signs and for seasons and for days and years, [15]and let them be lights in the dome of the sky to give light upon the earth." And it was so. [16]God made the two great lights—the greater light to rule the day and the lesser light to rule the night—and the stars. [17]God set them in the dome of the sky to give light upon the earth, [18]to rule over the day and over the night, and to separate the light from the darkness. And God saw that it was good. [19]And there was evening and there was morning, the fourth day.

[20]And God said, "Let the waters bring forth swarms of living creatures, and let birds fly above the earth across the dome of the sky." [21]So God created the great sea monsters and every living creature that moves, of every kind, with which the waters swarm, and every winged bird of every kind. And God saw that it was good. [22]God blessed them, saying, "Be fruitful and multiply and fill the waters in the seas, and let birds multiply on the earth." [23]And there was evening and there was morning, the fifth day.

[24]And God said, "Let the earth bring forth living creatures of every kind: cattle and creeping things and wild animals of the earth of every kind." And it was so. [25]God made the wild animals of the earth of every kind, and the cattle of every kind, and everything that creeps upon the ground of every kind. And God saw that it was good.

²⁶Then God said, "Let us make humankind in our image, according to our likeness; and let them have dominion over the fish of the sea, and over the birds of the air, and over the cattle, and over all the wild animals of the earth, and over every creeping thing that creeps upon the earth."

²⁷So God created humankind in his image,

in the image of God he created them;

male and female he created them.

²⁸God blessed them, and God said to them, "Be fruitful and multiply, and fill the earth and subdue it; and have dominion over the fish of the sea and over the birds of the air and over every living thing that moves upon the earth." ²⁹God said, "See, I have given you every plant yielding seed that is upon the face of all the earth, and every tree with seed in its fruit; you shall have them for food. ³⁰And to every beast of the earth, and to every bird of the air, and to everything that creeps on the earth, everything that has the breath of life, I have given every green plant for food." And it was so. ³¹God saw everything that he had made, and indeed, it was very good. And there was evening and there was morning, the sixth day.

GENESIS 2

Thus the heavens and the earth were finished, and all their multitude. ²And on the seventh day God finished the work that he had done, and he rested on the seventh day from all the work that he had done. ³So God blessed the seventh day and hallowed it, because on it God rested from all the work that he had done in creation.

⁴These are the generations of the heavens and the earth when they were created.

In the day that the Lord God made the earth and the heavens, ⁵when no plant of the field was yet in the earth and no herb of the field had yet sprung up—for the Lord God had not caused it to rain upon the earth, and there was no one to till the ground; ⁶but a stream would rise from the earth, and water the whole face of the ground—⁷then the Lord God formed man from the dust of the ground, and breathed into his nostrils the breath of life; and the man became a living being. ⁸And the Lord God planted a garden in Eden, in the east; and there he put the man whom he had formed. ⁹Out of the ground the Lord God made to grow every tree that is pleasant to the sight and good for food, the tree of life also in the midst of the garden, and the tree of the knowledge of good and evil.

¹⁰A river flows out of Eden to water the garden, and from there it divides and becomes four branches. ¹¹The name of the first is Pishon; it is the one that flows around the whole land of Havilah, where there is gold; ¹²and the gold of that land is good; bdellium and onyx stone are there. ¹³The name of the second river is Gihon; it is the one that flows around the whole land of Cush. ¹⁴The name of the third river is Tigris, which flows east of Assyria. And the fourth river is the Euphrates.

¹⁵The Lord God took the man and put him in the garden of Eden to till it and keep it. ¹⁶And the Lord God commanded the man, "You may freely eat of every tree of the garden; ¹⁷but of the tree of the knowledge of good and evil you shall not eat, for in the day that you eat of it you shall die."

¹⁸Then the Lord God said, "It is not good that the man should be alone; I will make him a helper as his partner." ¹⁹So out of the ground the Lord God formed every animal of the field and every bird of the air, and brought them to the man to see what he would call them; and whatever the man called every living creature, that was its name. ²⁰The man gave names to all cattle, and to the birds of the air, and to every animal of the field; but for the man there was not found a helper as his partner. ²¹So the Lord God caused a deep sleep to fall upon the

man, and he slept; then he took one of his ribs and closed up its place with flesh. ²²And the rib that the LORD God had taken from the man he made into a woman and brought her to the man. ²³Then the man said,

> "This at last is bone of my bones
> and flesh of my flesh;
> this one shall be called Woman,
> for out of Man this one was taken."

²⁴Therefore a man leaves his father and his mother and clings to his wife, and they become one flesh. ²⁵And the man and his wife were both naked, and were not ashamed.

GENESIS 3

Now the serpent was more crafty than any other wild animal that the LORD God had made. He said to the woman, "Did God say, 'You shall not eat from any tree in the garden'?" ²The woman said to the serpent, "We may eat of the fruit of the trees in the garden; ³but God said, 'You shall not eat of the fruit of the tree that is in the middle of the garden, nor shall you touch it, or you shall die.'" ⁴But the serpent said to the woman, "You will not die; ⁵for God knows that when you eat of it your eyes will be opened, and you will be like God, knowing good and evil." ⁶So when the woman saw that the tree was good for food, and that it was a delight to the eyes, and that the tree was to be desired to make one wise, she took of its fruit and ate; and she also gave some to her husband, who was with her, and he ate. ⁷Then the eyes of both were opened, and they knew that they were naked; and they sewed fig leaves together and made loincloths for themselves.

⁸They heard the sound of the LORD God walking in the garden at the time of the evening breeze, and the man and his wife hid themselves from the presence of the LORD God among the

trees of the garden. ⁹But the LORD God called to the man, and said to him, "Where are you?" ¹⁰He said, "I heard the sound of you in the garden, and I was afraid, because I was naked; and I hid myself." ¹¹He said, "Who told you that you were naked? Have you eaten from the tree of which I commanded you not to eat?" ¹²The man said, "The woman whom you gave to be with me, she gave me fruit from the tree, and I ate." ¹³Then the LORD God said to the woman, "What is this that you have done?" The woman said, "The serpent tricked me, and I ate." ¹⁴The LORD God said to the serpent,

> "Because you have done this,
>> cursed are you among all animals
>> and among all wild creatures;
> upon your belly you shall go,
>> and dust you shall eat
>> all the days of your life.
> ¹⁵I will put enmity between you and the woman,
>> and between your offspring and hers;
> he will strike your head,
>> and you will strike his heel."

¹⁶To the woman he said,

> "I will greatly increase your pangs in childbearing;
>> in pain you shall bring forth children,
> yet your desire shall be for your husband,
>> and he shall rule over you."

¹⁷And to the man he said,

> "Because you have listened to the voice of your wife,
>> and have eaten of the tree
> about which I commanded you,
>> 'You shall not eat of it,'
> cursed is the ground because of you;
>> in toil you shall eat of it all the days of your life;

¹⁸thorns and thistles it shall bring forth for you;
>   and you shall eat the plants of the field.
¹⁹By the sweat of your face
>   you shall eat bread
until you return to the ground,
>   for out of it you were taken;
you are dust,
>   and to dust you shall return."

²⁰The man named his wife Eve, because she was the mother of all living. ²¹And the LORD God made garments of skins for the man and for his wife, and clothed them.

²²Then the LORD God said, "See, the man has become like one of us, knowing good and evil; and now, he might reach out his hand and take also from the tree of life, and eat, and live forever"——²³therefore the LORD God sent him forth from the garden of Eden, to till the ground from which he was taken. ²⁴He drove out the man; and at the east of the garden of Eden he placed the cherubim, and a sword flaming and turning to guard the way to the tree of life.

CHAPTER 1

INTERPRETING THE CREATION STORIES

Since we are humans and not trees, we are compelled to be anthropomorphic rather than dendromorphic. The god of a tree will share in the image of a tree; our God will share in the image of a human.

—HAROLD BLOOM[1]

GENESIS is prefaced by two remarkable creation stories, from different authors and from different times. Such a claim from modern biblical scholarship means a rejection of an older view that the Bible begins with one creation story, written by Moses as he wrote the entire first five books. Although nothing in the text tells who the authors were, Mosaic authorship was presupposed because the account tells of his experiences with God in Egypt and on a mountainside in Sinai where rules were laid out for the people. It was further thought that God revealed to Moses how the world was created, a revelation Moses put at the beginning of his first book. And, for Christians, New Testament references to "the book of Moses" were evidence of Mosaic authorship.[2]

TWO DOCUMENTS—
THE PRIESTLY AND THE YAHWIST

The claim that there are two creation stories is related to what is called the Documentary Hypothesis. This hypothesis has been around for well over a century and in modified form is still widely accepted today in Christian and Jewish academic circles. The original hypothesis argued that the package of five books at the beginning of the Bible, called the Torah by Jews and the Pentateuch by many Christians, was produced by editors who collected and edited documents from several different earlier sources.

Based on linguistic clues in the text, along with inferences from how they refer to God, the documents or strands may now be reconstructed from the biblical text. They are identified as J (the Yahwist document), E (the Elohist), P (the Priestly) and D (the book of Deuteronomy). The reconstruction shows that two of the documents contained creation stories, giving us a Priestly creation story (P) and a Yahwist creation story (J). The P story is told in Genesis 1:1—2:4a, while J begins with Genesis 2:4b and continues to the end of chapter 3. Sections from J and P are mixed with E in the following chapters.

Who wrote these stories? Where and when were they written? Scholarly opinion varies somewhat on these questions, but some broad judgments may be made. The Yahwist story is the oldest, coming from someone familiar with farm life in Palestine and writing in the tenth or ninth century BCE. It is Israel's first written history and coincided with the rule of David or Solomon. The Priestly story, written later, is a preface to the extensive later passages involving the role of priests. It reflects urban life and was written during the time of the Babylonian exile or soon after, in the sixth or fifth century BCE.[3] Authors? A priest or priests for P, certainly a man. Probably not a priest for J, although beyond that, little may be surmised except that the author was a talented person. J probably also was a man, although there are at least two who allow for the possibility of female authorship.[4]

With this background, we look now to the stories themselves. A careful reading reveals a number of differences and even contradictions between the two, differences that relate to the controversies that will be considered in later chapters. Here is an overview.

COMPARING J AND P—
THE NAME OF GOD

In the Hebrew text, the older Yahwist story of creation consistently uses the special name for the god of the Israelites, YHWH, which is usually written Yahweh because this is the way it probably was pronounced.[5] This story is thus called the Yahwist and may easily be compared with the Priestly story where the name Yahweh is never found. Translators usually follow the Jewish practice of not using the holy name Yahweh, so the word is not found in most English Bibles. There is a substitute word, usually LORD, and when LORD appears, the original is Yahweh. Thus, in Genesis 2:4b, the NRSV says "In the day the LORD God made the heavens and the earth," and we know that LORD God translates Yahweh God. Since this is the first time Yahweh is used, we know the Yahwist story has begun.

The Priestly story uses only the word *Elohim*, which is "God" in English translations. Certainly the priests knew the holy name Yahweh, so why did they not say that Yahweh created all things? The holy name is a complex issue, and the name has a special term in scholarly circles, "the Tetragrammaton."[6] From what is known, usage of the name changed in the centuries between J and P. The name came to be considered so holy it was reserved for very special occasions and was not written in most documents, so *Elohim* was used instead of *Yahweh* in the Priestly story.

COMPARING J AND P—
WHAT EXISTED BEFORE CREATION?

According to most of Christian and Jewish tradition, before the creation, nothing existed except God, so God created the world out of nothing (the Latin *creatio ex nihilo* is often used). A careful reading of Genesis shows that this is not what the two creation stories say. Most scholars agree that creation out of nothing is a later idea and is not found in the Scriptures before 2 Maccabees 7:28, an apocryphal book of the first century BCE: "I beseech you, my child, to look at the heaven and the earth and see everything that is in them, and recognize that God did not make them out of things that existed."

The Genesis stories both start with God and something. According to the Priestly account, before the creation there were (a) God and (b) waters. The NRSV translation starts with *"when* God created," encouraging us to understand the first two verses as a preface describing conditions before creation. This preface says that "darkness covered the face of the deep" and "a wind[7] from God swept over the face of the waters," implying a preexisting watery world. Since creation is by the voice of God in chapter 1, the creative activity does not begin until "God said" in verse 3.

The waters in the Priestly story represent a preexisting chaos in the midst of which God creates. This watery chaos is pushed aside but remains and returns later as punishment in the story of the flood. There are two flood stories in Genesis, as there are two creation stories, one from the Priestly account and one from the Yahwist, although the final editor has scrambled the two and they are not as easy to separate as the creation stories. The J flood story says simply that it rained for forty days. The P story both in the creation and in the flood understands that our world exists in the midst of waters, and so in the flood "the fountains of the great deep burst forth, and the windows of the heavens were opened" (Gen 7:11).[8]

A preexisting watery world is found in many cultures. Today we have dozens of creation stories from all over the world, and many of these picture a watery universe in the midst of which the sun, moon, earth, and living creatures came into existence. Some picture an egg floating on the waters, with life beginning in the egg and eventually breaking out. A few are "earth diver" stories of how some creature floating on the waters learned to dive deep enough to bring up soil with which to form an island. The Babylonian story, which was familiar to the Israelites and which probably had some influence on the Priestly story, pictures a great cosmic struggle on the waters between the male god Marduk and his female protagonist Tiamat, a violent struggle in which Marduk slays Tiamat and from her body makes the heavens and the earth.[9]

The picture of a world created in the midst of the waters would be obvious to earlier people. Water is in all directions— it is above (rain comes down), below (dig down and find it), and on all sides (go anywhere and land eventually meets water). Or there may be a psychological reason for seeing water as a starting point—the waters of creation stories may reflect a hidden memory of the waters of the womb, our first home.

The Yahwist story is quite different, for before creation there were (a) the LORD God and (b) earth. At the beginning, "the LORD God had not caused it to rain upon the earth, and there was no one to till the ground" (Gen 2:5). Reflecting the experience of early farmers, the story is earth-based. At the beginning there was earth waiting for the LORD God to create green plants and to bring rain and also waiting for humans to cooperate by farming the arable ground.

Water or *earth*. Even though later tradition has spoken of *creatio ex nihilo*, the creation stories tell of something existing before the creation. There is discussion today about whether *creatio ex nihilo* should still be championed, with some environ- mentalists and feminists saying it should be abandoned. Critics of the idea say God and world are interdependent, and there never was a time when there was nothing.[10] The creation stories offer an opening here, for with earth and water the stories tell of some "stuff" of the universe existing before God began to create.

COMPARING J AND P— GOD, SEX, AND CREATION

A common theme in creation stories around the world is that gods create by having sex. Father Sun joins with Mother Earth for some of the American Indians, Izanagi and Izanami unite in sexual embrace for the Japanese, Yang and Yin are cosmic forces whose dynamic interaction brings all things into being for the Chinese. The *Kama Sutra* is a famous Hindu sex manual, describing husband and wife as echoing the gods and goddesses in their coital bed. For the Canaanite neighbors of the Israelites, fertility in its various forms was dependent on the Baals, the gods who regularly had sex with their consorts the Asheroth.[11] For almost all earlier people, sex meant creation.

Remarkably, the two Genesis stories stand as exceptions to this nearly universal theme. *The God of Genesis does not create by sex*. On this the two stories agree.

Here is seen an unfolding drama. The writers of the Pen- tateuch would like us to think that the Israelites were mostly worshippers of their great god Yahweh. But in reality, the people lived in a culturally diverse area and many were poly-theists. They intermarried with other peoples and regularly as-sociated with neighbors and passing traders who worshipped a variety of gods and goddesses.[12] Moses and the leaders during those early times usually recognized other gods while also say-ing Yahweh alone should be worshipped. Note the opening of the Decalogue, "I am the LORD your God . . . you shall have no other gods before me" (Exod 20:2-3). The existence of these other gods and goddesses was taken for granted by many, and some of the people of Israel found them appealing. Thus the Pentateuch is polemical, supporting Yahweh alone and arguing against the others.

Much of the appeal of the other gods was that they had to do with sex and fertility, something missing in the worship of Yahweh. To be successful—in having sons or in raising grain or in keeping sheep—one must turn to specialists in fertility, to the Baals and the Asheroth.[13] Sacred prostitution was found at some of the shrines, a practice with obvious appeal to some of the men of Israel. David and Solomon and some of the later kings were part of the picture, for they set up altars for the gods and goddesses of their foreign wives. Solomon even sup-ported worship of strange gods in the temple of Yahweh in Je-rusalem, and King Josiah later removed from the holy temple the vessels dedicated to Baal and Asherah.[14] The prophet Hosea railed against the worship of these gods and goddesses and ap-parently married a woman, Gomer, who may have been a sa-cred prostitute in service to Baal.

Advocates of the worship of Yahweh had the task of per-suading the people that their God was different and superior. The primary difference was that Yahweh was the God of the exodus from Egypt—the God who chooses a people, promises a homeland, and establishes a covenant; the God who provides laws to guide human conduct and is concerned with world leaders and the life of nations. The other gods and goddesses were manifestations of nature, and since sex is imbedded in nature, these deities were sexual beings. But this God Yahweh was not, as we say now, a God of nature but of history. Just as history transcends nature and is not sexual, Yahweh transcends nature and is not sexual.[15]

God in Genesis is not "he" or "she" and may not be symbolized with penis or womb, symbols that are found in many other religions.[16] God creates by speaking (nonsexual), by forming or breathing (nonsexual). Although described in the Hebrew language that uses "he," this God is neither male nor female but a God beyond gender. Here is a God with a very different relationship to the natural world than the other gods. Sex is not in the nature of this God; sex is not a preexisting cosmic force that is the instrument for all creation. Instead, sex is created by this God. In chapter 2 we will consider feminist discussions of this theme and the desire of some to speak again of mothering qualities of God. We also will see in chapter 3 that some scholars concerned with the environment think that the perspectives of "primitive," nature-affirming religions (represented in the Bible by the Baals and the Asheroth) had something important to say and that we should reconsider the biblical rejection.

COMPARING J AND P— CHOOSING HUMAN TRAITS

Religious traditions have mostly spoken of gods as like persons, and not as "its" or impersonal forces. For us humans, the only person we know is a human person, so God is described as being like a human. The term for this is *anthropomorphism*, the use of human traits to describe God. Which human traits will be chosen? God cannot have sexual traits, so that part of human experience must be avoided and the choice of other human traits must be made carefully. P and J are both insightful in their anthropomorphic descriptions.

"Then God said, 'Let there be light.'" *And God said . . . and God said . . . and God said . . .* This speaking by God is repeated over and over in ritual fashion during the six days. We must surmise that on the seventh day when God rested, God must have rested his voice! The emphasis on the power of God's spoken words reflects the outlook of priests whose lives and religion focused on words, spoken and written. The anthropomorphic description is a nonsexual trait that humans share with God and not with other creatures, for only God and humans use words. Genesis 1 stands at the beginning of a long tradition in Judaism, Christianity, and Islam that focuses on sacred written words and upon a God who relates to humans through words.[17] It is a distinctive characteristic of the Priestly account and sets it apart from the Yahwist.[18]

The anthropomorphism of the Yahwist account is different. In J the LORD God forms man from the dust of the ground (a potter with dirty hands) and breathes into his nostrils (breath meaning life). The LORD God then plants (a horticulturist), opens the man's side (a surgeon), walks (a watchman), and carries on a conversation (a companion)—all of which activity is absent from the Priestly telling. The anthropomorphism of the Yahwist is colorful, down to earth, and dramatic. It pictures Yahweh within the created world, doing a variety of things humans do.

We may say the Yahwist pictures a God who is imminent, while the Priestly picture is of a transcendent God. Words transcend their environment, they float above the natural world, they may be free and spontaneous, and they are supernatural—all of which is true of God in the Priestly story. By contrast, Yahweh in the J account is immanent, as the story pictures Yahweh on the earth and in the garden, a God who is never above but always in the creation. These contrasting views of God will be considered in chapter 3, where environmental theologians debate the relationship of God with the natural world.

COMPARING J AND P—MEN AND WOMEN

What the two Genesis stories say about man and woman will be the focus of our next chapter, so we will not go into detail here. In brief, however, note that the Priestly story in Genesis 1 tells how God created them "male and female," implying that man and woman were created at the same time. Then Genesis 2 starts over and tells it differently. For the Yahwist, man is created first, then living things and a garden are created so the man will have a place to live. Finally, the woman is created to be a helper to the man.

In the next chapter we will see that the traditional reading of the Yahwist account becomes a focus of much of feminism's complaint about the Bible. The Priestly story's treatment of man and woman comes off rather well, but there are other feminist concerns about P.

ANDROGYNY AND 'ADAM IN J

The original human being, according to Plato, was in three forms—male-female, male-male, and female-female. Then, early on, a splitting occurred, and since then each human is half a person, looking for the other half.[19] This myth of the androgyn (male-female) is found in a number of cultures and is prominent in India, where Hinduism speaks of the union and then separation of Hindu gods and goddesses, such as Shiva-

Shakti. A visit to major art museums is likely to reveal Hindu statues presenting male and female in one form.

Some think the Yahwist story tells of an androgynous human. The first human, 'adam, was a combination of male and female, and there was no separate man until the woman appeared, the rib representing the splitting of the original androgynous 'adam into male and female.[20] Others hold a similar but slightly different view, arguing that 'adam originally was neither male nor female but nongendered, so that male and female were not in the original human but appeared first when the rib was removed.[21]

Most scholars reject the androgyny claim and think the Yahwist is saying clearly that the man was created first, and the woman last. But androgyny adds an interesting twist and has a clear advantage for a feminist reading—the man and the woman appear at the same time, as in the Priestly story, removing the traditional interpretation that the woman was created later and thus had secondary status.

SEX AND SIN IN J

God is not a sexual being, but the man and the woman decidedly are. So no overview of the Yahwist story may sidestep this issue. To put it plainly, does the forbidden fruit mean sex? And does the story say that the woman seduced the man and that seduction was her special guilt?

The story does suggest sex. The man and woman at first were naked and not ashamed. But then they disobeyed and were ashamed, so the LORD God made garments for them, seemingly to cover their disobedient parts. If they were ashamed of their disobedient parts, why did they wear loincloths and not gloves and masks? And could the snake be a phallic symbol as the woman was awakening sexually? The man and the woman seem like teens undergoing a rite of passage, as they discover their sexuality and behave as teens sometimes do, disobeying a strong father who has laid down the law.

"Adam, Eve, and the serpent" has been a theme for countless Jewish and Christian leaders, thinkers, and artists through the centuries as they have struggled to address sexuality, marriage, and childbearing.[22] This part of the story has been a kind of Rorschach test and has brought forth endless commentaries and interpretations. It was a hot topic in the first centuries of Christianity, with many views and counterviews expressed in an ongoing debate. The leader who came to stand above others in influence was Augustine of Hippo (354–430). His view is vilified by many feminists[23] and relates to our next chapter, so let us introduce it here.

Augustine argued that Adam and Eve were created good and had remarkable freedom, but they made a tragic mistake. In their disobedience they introduced sin, so their disobedience has affected all humans since (and, of course, for him, the woman bears the greater guilt). We are thus from our mothers' wombs infected with original sin. Adam and Eve had a choice to be good, but all later humans have no choice. They are sinful by nature. In his interpretation Augustine was drawing upon a statement in a letter of St. Paul, "For just as by the one man's [Adam's] disobedience the many were made sinners, so by the one man's [Christ's] obedience the many will be made righteous" (Rom 5:19).

What about sex? God did tell the first pair to be fruitful and multiply, so sex in itself is not sinful, and the first pair could have had sex and produced children without sin. But because we are so contaminated by sin, sex as humans know it today is especially tainted, according to Augustine. The problem is the strong desire that controls sex, for the sex organs are so intent on their own satisfaction they are impossible to control.[24] Augustine writes in Latin, and *libido* is his word, a word that means desire or lust. Since sex is so tainted by *libido*, semen and the uncontrollable passion of sex become the vehicles through which original sin is passed through the generations.[25]

Most branches of Christianity count original sin as a significant teaching to describe a universal condition of human brokenness. While almost no one today supports Augustine's interpretation of how sin is transmitted from generation to generation, Augustine's connection of sin to sex continues to trouble Christianity. There have been within the last century various efforts to overcome a history of negative attitudes toward sex, but this is an area where problems continue to trouble the churches.

Judaism does not like this talk about original sin, instead speaking of *yetzer hara*, an inclination to do evil found alike in the first pair and in humans today. Sex does not carry any special weight in this inclination, for sex was created by God to be good. Marriage and family are central in Judaism, and the inclination to do evil sometimes results in adultery, with King David often cited as an example. Sex in marriage is encouraged, and there is no tradition of celibacy. In fact, one of the Jewish commandments is for husband and wife to have sex on the Sabbath, thinking of this as a holy act on a holy day.[26]

A DOME AND THE WORLD OF P

Talk of sin and sex relates to the Yahwist story. Views of the universe refer mostly to the Priestly source, to which we now turn. The NRSV has for Genesis 1:6-7, "And God said, 'Let there be a *dome* in the midst of the waters, and let it separate the waters from the waters (emphasis added).' . . . And it was so. God called the dome Sky." The NIV speaks not of dome but

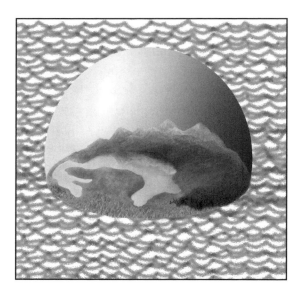

CREATION AT THE END OF DAY 3

Light is separated from darkness, a dome is in the midst of the waters, dry land and seas may be seen, and there is vegetation. The dome is empty because sun and moon will be created on day 4. Creatures of the land, sea, and sky will be created on days 5 and 6, and humans at the end of day 6. Artist interpretation by Catherine Jennings.

of *vault*, while the RSV follows the older King James and uses *firmament*. A contemporary Jewish translation, TANAKH, has *expanse*.

Dome, vault, firmament, expanse: The original Hebrew word implied a bowl of hammered metal. The image suggests a bell or a tent or a roof, a partition in the midst of the cosmic waters in anticipation of what will be created next.[27] With all that water, a dome means a dry space as a starting point.

The next step is to call forth dry land in the midst of the waters. Here we begin to get a picture of what the story is describing. It is a world with two levels—our earth and then a sky-world above where gods live and where the heavenly bodies make their appointed rounds. The biblical authors shared this picture of a two-leveled world with other people of their era, as part of a commonsense understanding of how the world operates.[28] Although nowhere does the Bible actually say the earth is flat, the implication of the Priestly story is that the earth is a flat sphere with a domelike expanse above, all surrounded by the cosmic waters.

The sun and moon and stars are created late—after the earth and vegetation—for there must first be a dome in which to put them and an earth that they are to look down on. Note the unusual order. Light and a separation of day and night are called forth in day one when all that exists is God and water. Then comes the dome (day two), the earth and vegetation (day three), and the sun (not until day four).

The view of the world in the Priestly story is in many ways different from modern views, influenced so much by the discoveries of Nicolaus Copernicus, by the explosion of scientific knowledge, and by space exploration. With this tension between ancient and modern, a bag of tangled issues has been opened, issues that will be addressed in some detail in our chapter 4.

BIBLICAL CRITICISM AND SCHOLARLY APPROACHES TO THE BIBLE

"Biblical criticism" is the broad category that covers the approach to the Bible that we are using.[29] "Criticism" comes from a Greek word that means discernment or rational analysis essential for a deeper understanding of a complex subject. The work of a good biblical critic is akin to that of a drama critic, a literary critic, an art critic, and it may lead to enriched appreciation. The common understanding of criticism as faultfinding is far from the meaning here.

This approach grew out of the eighteenth-century Enlightenment—with its humanism, fascination with history, and encouragement of early science—and developed considerably in the nineteenth and twentieth centuries. True to this background, biblical criticism has attempted to focus on the Bible as a human book and to read without the influence of dogmas or traditional interpretations. It draws on human sciences—such as philology, archaeology, history—and has at times attempted to be scientific and objective in approaching the Bible.[30]

"Historical criticism" and "the historical-critical method" are other terms often used, focusing on such questions as who was the author and when did he (or she) write, what influences came to bear on the writing, did events being described actually take place, when and how did the various sections of the text come to be put together, how does one text differ from another? Our analysis of the two creation stories in this chapter draws upon this approach.

While historical criticism is still widely used, some biblical critics today find that as a scholarly approach, it has limitations, and so they wish to move ahead with new approaches. Biblical criticism is a big umbrella that describes a dynamic field with a sometimes confusing mix of approaches—historical criticism (still), textual criticism, form criticism, source criticism, redaction criticism, social-scientific criticism, and others. These various approaches come up mostly where full-time specialists in biblical studies discuss things with other specialists, so they will not be central to our study. But they do play a role at places, so let us note briefly how they relate to our next three chapters.

Chapter 3 and its discussion of environmental issues will find only a few who are specialists in biblical studies. Certainly today's biblical scholarship would be accepted by most who enter into the debates, but the more specialized types of biblical criticism do not weigh in most of the discussions.

Chapter 4 will be different, for in this chapter we will see a vigorous creationist attack against biblical criticism, especially against the historical-critical method. This attack is the latest in a century-old struggle against modern biblical scholarship by those who identify themselves as fundamentalists. We will discuss both fundamentalist objections to how biblical critics handle the Genesis stories and also the defense of biblical criticism by mainline churches.

Chapter 2 also will deal with scholars who specialize in a study of the Bible, but in this chapter the struggle will be not between fundamentalists and biblical critics, but between feminist biblical critics and the male-dominated ways of reading the Bible (including much of the biblical criticism of the past century).[31] We will discuss Phyllis Trible, a feminist biblical critic who is well known for her treatment of the J story, so let us note her method to illustrate the variety of approaches. Her method is "rhetorical criticism" and is part of a concern for the Bible as literature that has grown in importance.[32] Trible does not reject the historical-critical method but chooses to do something different. She focuses on the Hebrew text of the J story as it is written in its final form, with no attention to items that come up in historical criticism, such as a concern about the history of the text or a comparison with P.

Biblical criticism and its various approaches illustrate the freedom many Jews and Christians today exhibit as they approach the biblical text. The Bible is human, it has limitations, it at times disagrees with itself, it champions things that today we do not like. Some Jews and Christians now feel free to say the Bible cannot stand as the final authority in some areas; it must be augmented or even challenged. Again, the three areas in our study are illustrative. For feminists, women's experiences must stand as a judge of the Bible and its patriarchy. For some environmentalists, an appreciation for the natural world must be developed from outside the Bible and then brought to the Bible because the Bible's views are inadequate. For those convinced of the accuracy of evolutionary theories, an insightful view of the universe is developing out of science and must be used in interpreting the Bible. In all three areas something outside the Bible, some insight or knowledge or authority, is brought to bear in interpreting the Bible.

BIBLICAL CRITICISM
AND QUESTIONS OF BIBLICAL AUTHORITY

Before the development of biblical criticism, the dominant view was that the Bible came from God as a divine oracle.[33] The Bible came to us through humans, yes, but its ultimate source was beyond the human in the mind of God, who moved the authors to write these pages. For Jews, God inspired Moses to write the Torah. Christians have thought both testaments to be inspired and have commonly spoken of the Bible as the Word of God. It followed, then, that the faithful were called upon to accept all the Bible says. This divine oracle view is still widely held and not just in fundamentalist circles. Obviously it clashes with many presuppositions of biblical criticism.

Does the Bible still have authority and meaning for those who accept biblical criticism, and if so, in what ways? These questions are greatly troubling for many who feel they cannot return to a simpler divine oracle perspective. Many Jews and Christians who approach the Bible critically still in some sense think of the Bible as inspired, but they look for fresh insights about the mode of inspiration. It is indeed a very human book, but in this book is the story of humans who wrestled with important questions and who came to know God through this wrestling. God is known to us not through a divine oracle but through the stories and testimonies recorded in this book. The emphasis is not on the words themselves but on the people's experiences of the divine that the Bible has recorded. Almost all who accept a critical approach to the Bible still say the Bible is a special book with continuing meaning and authority and that reading the Bible is very different from reading a daily newspaper. No Christian calls for changing "the Word of God" to the more accurate "the words of Israelite scribes and early Christians."[34]

Many today would say the Bible in itself, as a book lying on a table, has no meaning or authority. The Bible comes alive as people in a community of faith engage it. It is the Jewish people's Torah, it is the church's Bible—meaning and faith may unfold as people earnestly engage these ancient writings.[35] Feminist approaches serve as an excellent example, for some feminists say that a Bible lying on the table is truly alien and harmful to women, so the first impulse is to reject it. But women, in community with other women and supportive men, may read and find that some of the Bible can become powerful and liberating for women. In the process the Bible can become holy scripture and its authority can grow out of the process of wrestling with its pages.[36]

These issues are reflected in the ways Jews and Christians today approach their two creation stories. Perhaps they are still meaningful as they are written and carry insights that are often missed. Or perhaps there are problems with the stories that are so basic that the stories should be replaced by new stories or augmented with insights from outside the Bible. The new freedom to interpret the text has produced serious challenges, and these challenges are being dealt with as communities of faith read and discuss the stories.

FUNDAMENTALIST REACTIONS
TO BIBLICAL CRITICISM

Fundamentalism as a movement solidified in the early twentieth century in the United States to defend its own divine oracle view of the Bible and to do battle against the inroads being made by biblical criticism. Two events were significant in fundamentalism's beginning, the first being the affirmation of the Five Points by the northern Presbyterian Church in 1910, building upon action taken as early as 1893. The other event was the publication of a series of twelve booklets called *The Fundamentals*, issued between 1910 and 1914 and distributed in the millions free of charge.

Central to the Five Points and to *The Fundamentals* was the assertion that the Bible is "without error," the principle of inerrancy. Against the developing biblical criticism, fundamentalists argued that God is the true author of the Bible and what we read is without error. Inerrancy covers matters of faith and salvation, of course, but it also includes events in history, such as the long lives of the patriarchs and the biblical miracles. And, in a theme central for a consideration of creationism, inerrancy means the Bible is read literally and Genesis describes accurately God's created world and how it came into being.[37]

With the emphasis on inerrancy, we see why fundamentalism was born as a reaction against biblical criticism. As the new approach to understanding the Bible gained acceptance in most Protestant denominations and their seminaries and colleges, many conservatives reacted with alarm because they felt that the very authority of Christianity's beloved Bible was being undermined. Interpretations of Genesis were (and continue to be) at the heart of much of the concern, and the authors of *The Fundamentals* spent more time on the opening chapters of Genesis than on any other part of the Bible. The argument that there are two creation stories in the Bible and that the Pentateuch is a human document that contains material that may not be accurate brought forceful responses. If these opening chapters of the Bible cannot be trusted, many thought, then nothing else in the Bible may be trusted. It was time to take a stand, to declare confidence in the Bible. Fundamentalists were angry and militant. And they still are as they take up the creationist cause.

How many Americans are fundamentalists today? A Gallup Poll in 2006 found 28 percent saying, "The Bible is the actual word of God and is to be taken literally." Even though the figure is high, it is not as high as it has been. The Gallup organization has been asking this question for years and has documented a steady decline in fundamentalist commitment. Gallup found 37 to 40 percent to be biblical literalists in the years 1976 to 1984 and a remarkable 65 percent in 1963.[38]

BIBLICAL CRITICISM IN THE CHURCHES

For most Protestant denominations, the fundamentalist controversy was settled decades ago as biblical criticism came to be increasingly accepted in Europe and America. Clergy and many laypeople today are familiar with methods of Bible study that emphasize historical development, and they commonly talk about J and E and P when reading the first books of the Bible. Even the Presbyterians, who once adopted the Five Points, have changed their minds and now reject inerrancy and champion biblical criticism.[39] Our analysis of Genesis in this chapter would be acceptable in the mainline Protestant denominations—

Methodist, ELCA Lutheran, Presbyterian, Episcopal, American Baptist, United Church of Christ, and others.[40]

Of the major Protestant denominations, the most prominent ones that are fundamentalist in their teachings are the Southern Baptist Convention and the Lutheran Church—Missouri Synod. There are also smaller denominations and quite a few independent churches that are fundamentalist.

What about the Roman Catholic Church? For decades biblical criticism and the Documentary Hypothesis were officially rejected by the Roman Catholic Church, which continued to support Mosaic authorship and was suspicious of work done by Protestant scholars. For example, in 1910 a professor at Catholic University, Henry Poels, was dismissed for supporting the hypothesis.[41]

Then a sea change occurred within Catholic scholarship. In 1943 Pope Pius XII issued an encyclical, *Divino Afflante Spiritu*, which supported the new scholarly methods of biblical study and in important ways anticipated the Second Vatican Council of the 1960's. As an indication of the change, *The Jerome Bible Commentary*, an important work by Catholic scholars published in 1968, enthusiastically supported the Documentary Hypothesis.[42] Today Protestants and Catholics share views and methods in biblical study, and usually it is difficult to tell from what religious community a biblical scholar comes.

While there is wide acceptance of biblical criticism at official levels in the churches, it should also be recognized that there is in both Protestant and Catholic circles a good bit of indifference to scholarly work and even some anti-intellectualism. The insights of leading biblical scholars may be far removed from the views of many churchgoers and from the thinking of some clergy. Fundamentalism and other conservative or reactionary viewpoints often are at home not just in churches that are self-proclaimed fundamentalist, but in other churches as well.

JUDAISM AND BIBLICAL SCHOLARSHIP

Jewish scholars in their understanding of the Torah are generally as supportive of the view that the Torah came from earlier collected traditions as are their Christian counterparts.[43] However, in the more conservative Judaism where rabbis work within synagogues, the picture is complex. The centrality of the Torah is manifest in the scroll that is the focus of Sabbath worship and study, and the tradition is that the Torah is a unified revelation from God. To say that many authors, several sources, and centuries of development lie back of the Torah is a serious challenge to some. So Mosaic authorship and its one creation story are still supported in some traditional Jewish circles.[44] Even so, the Jewish approach is not simple.

In speaking of Mosaic authorship, the Jewish tradition says that on the mountain God gave Moses both the Torah and the Oral Torah. The Torah may not be understood apart from this Oral Torah, which has extended throughout Jewish history and been captured in such documents as the Talmud and in the lively and continuing debates among rabbis. The Torah is thus not understood through its words alone but is read in the light of the long and living history of Jewish interpretations of the Torah. This makes even traditional Judaism quite different from Protestant fundamentalism, with its emphasis on a literal reading of a fact-filled text.

CONCLUSION

In this opening chapter, our focus has been on separate and parallel stories in the book of Genesis. Using insights developed from biblical criticism, the two stories have been analyzed and compared in order to highlight their similarities and differences. The stories stand separately and may not be harmonized without doing an injustice to each. The Bible presents variety, and we are richer for it.

Yet even though the two stories are separate, they may not be separated. The two belong together, for they are part of one Bible and one tradition. They relate to each other; they are in conversation with each other; they supplement each other. In the following chapters, we will see how feminists, environmentalists, and creationists address the creation stories, and how the stories respond in their own words or through the voices of their interpreters. We begin a dialogue with the two creation stories, just as they dialogue with each other.

CHAPTER 2

GENESIS AND THE CHALLENGES OF FEMINISTS

The Genesis report of the creation of women is still as bristling with mysteries as a porcupine with quills.
—THEODORE REIK[1]

ELIZABETH CADY STANTON is widely heralded by feminists for her early and clear recognition of the harm to women that comes from the patriarchal traditions of Christianity and its Bible. *The Woman's Bible*, edited by her and published in 1898, attempted to show which parts of the Bible are positive for women and which sections are hopelessly biased and therefore to be rejected.

Stanton recognized that there are two creation stories in Genesis and saw that what we call the Priestly account presents woman as equal to man in status. This account goes even further by giving clear support for a heavenly Mother, according to Stanton.

If language has any meaning, we have in these texts a
plain declaration of the existence of the feminine element
in the Godhead, equal in power and glory with the masculine. The Heavenly Mother and Father! "God created
man in his own image, male and female."[2]

Stanton then argued that the story in Genesis 2 and 3 treats
woman in a tragically different way. Man is the first to be created and woman is treated as an afterthought, an inferior creature who brings sin into the world. What we call the Yahwist
account must be rejected.[3]

The Woman's Bible introduces us to two key questions. Is
the Priestly account positive (or perhaps negative) in its views
toward women? And is the Yahwist account negative (or perhaps positive)? Our task in this chapter is to see what Jewish
and Christian feminist scholars say to these questions.[4]

FEMINIST PROBLEMS
WITH THE BIBLE

In the days of Elizabeth Cady Stanton and her supporters, almost all Jewish and Christian scholarship was done by men,
men who were largely blind to the problems the Bible might
present for women. But since the 1960s there has been an explosion in the number of women scholars in religion, and today
hundreds of women have developed careers in biblical scholarship and related fields, with a large number considering themselves feminist. These women are at the forefront of biblical
study, publishing many of the most influential volumes in their
field and holding prestigious teaching positions. Now mainstream, their influence is growing among both female and male
scholars, and no serious biblical scholarship is possible today
without attention to what feminists are saying.

For most Jewish and Christian feminists, the Bible is a "dangerous book."[5] They agree with Elizabeth Cady Stanton that this is a book that in many ways has done harm to women. Phyllis Trible expresses the problem for women:

> I face a terrible dilemma: Choose ye this day whom you will serve: the God of the fathers or the God of sisterhood. If the God of the fathers, then the Bible supplies models for your slavery. If the God of sisterhood, then you must reject patriarchal religion and go forth without models to claim your freedom.

Yet while the Bible presents major problems for women, it is not to be totally rejected. Trible continues:

> The more I participate in the [feminist] Movement, the more I discover my freedom through the appropriation of biblical symbols. . . . There is another way; to reread (not rewrite) the Bible without the blinders of Israelite men or of Paul, Barth, Bonhoeffer, and a host of others.[6]

Women may read the Bible, but they must read cautiously and critically. Elizabeth Schüssler Fiorenza suggests a "hermeneutics of suspicion."[7] Biblical texts must be read with great care, like an investigator would examine a crime scene where violence against women has been done. A cover-up must always be suspected, and women must suspect a cover-up for harmful male dominance throughout the Bible.[8]

Being suspicious toward the Bible, Jewish and Christian feminists reject parts of the Bible but do not reject it all. The Bible is the foundational document for the traditions and faiths with which they identify, and there are many feminists who draw inspiration from the Bible. Plus, in solidarity with millions of women through the ages, especially poor women today and women of color, feminists recognize that the Bible has often been powerful and meaningful to women. The Bible, in spite of its faults, should be read carefully and without the male biases that have influenced interpretations for centuries. In their reading, feminists focus on those sections positive for women, creating a "canon within the canon," an approach that has often been used by male readers.[9] Included in this canon are the prophetic elements that talk of liberating the oppressed and creating a new day of hope, biblical themes also found in third-world liberation theology and in black theology. Included also are female images of God, as will be seen later in this chapter.

How does one judge what in the Bible falls under feminist suspicion and what is included in the feminist canon? Do the two creation stories get included? In making these judgments, *the primary criterion is the experience of women.* Rosemary Radford Ruether speaks for many feminists when she argues that whatever promotes "the full humanity of women" is of the holy and reflects an authentic relation to the divine, while what diminishes the full humanity of women does not reflect the divine and must be rejected. This new focus on the experience of women is a "grace event" according to Ruether, an insightful new way of interpreting the Bible.[10] For some it is disturbing to propose something out of human experience to judge a book considered holy, but as we noted in chapter 1, biblical criticism supports new freedom in dealing with the Bible, which itself is the product of human experience.

TRADITIONAL USES
OF THE YAHWIST STORY

Our analysis starts with the Yahwist account, for it is the one that receives most attention from feminists. Genesis 2 and 3 have been used countless times to show the inferiority and weakness of women, and it is not difficult to see why many from Elizabeth Cady Stanton to the present have rejected the story. Here is how the story has been understood:

- The man is created first and thus has higher standing. The woman is created last and is lower and inferior.
- Woman is created to be man's helpmate.
- Woman is the rib of man, derived from him and dependent on him.
- Woman is tempted by the serpent because she is weaker. The serpent knew better than to approach the stronger man.
- Woman was the first to sin, introducing sin and death to humanity.
- Woman's pain in childbearing is punishment because woman's guilt is greater than that of man.
- Woman is named by man. Naming shows the man's responsibility for ruling over her. Thus still today a woman takes her husband's name.

Since these interpretations of the Yahwist account serve as the entrenched foundation of Western views of women, in line with this foundation come statements from some of the leading male thinkers in Judaism and Christianity. Again a list, this time a litany of references often cited by feminists, all drawing upon the Yahwist story.

Paul in the New Testament. In giving advice on the question of whether men or women should cover their heads when praying, Paul says women should but men should not.[11] He cites Genesis 2.

For a man ought not to have his head veiled, since he is the image and reflection of God; but woman is the reflection of man. Indeed, man was not made from woman, but woman from man. Neither was man created for the sake of woman, but woman for the sake of man. (1 Cor 11:7-9)

A New Testament letter to Timothy. Citing Genesis 2, the argument is that women should not be leaders:

Let a woman learn in silence with full submission. I permit no women to teach or to have authority over a man; she is to keep silent. For Adam was formed first, then Eve; and Adam was not deceived, but the woman was deceived and became a transgressor. Yet she will be saved through childbearing, provided they continue in faith and love and holiness, with modesty. (1 Tim 2:11-15)

Most Christians ignore this today, while some supporters of Paul are happy to argue that Paul did not write it. Some Protestant conservatives quote this passage in saying women should not be pastors.

Tertullian. One of the most influential of the church fathers was the second-century theologian Tertullian. His became the common view that it was because of Eve's weakness that sin and death entered the world. And further, every woman today is a sister of Eve and thus "the devil's gateway."

And do you women not know that you are each an Eve? The sentence of God on this sex of yours lives in this age. . . . You are the devil's gateway; you are the unsealer of that forbidden tree; you are the first deserter of the divine law; you are she who persuaded him whom the devil was not valiant enough to attack. You destroyed so easily God's image, man. On account of your desert—that is, death—even the Son of God had to die.[12]

Thomas Aquinas. The dominant thinker in the Roman Catholic Church well into the modern era, Thomas in the thirteenth century reformulated the medieval view that the primary purpose of sex and marriage is to produce children. Women were created to help men make babies:

> It was necessary for women to be made, as the Scripture says, as a helper to man; not indeed as a helpmate in other works, as some say, since man can be more efficiently helped by another man in other works; but as a helper in the work of generation.[13]

Martin Luther. The Protestant reformers followed earlier Christian leaders in their interpretation of Genesis. Here, from Martin Luther:

> Hence it follows that if the woman had not been deceived by the serpent and had not sinned, she would have been the equal of Adam in all respects. For the punishment, that she is now subjected to the man, was imposed on her after sin and because of sin. . . . Eve was not like the woman of today, her state was far better and she was in no respect inferior to Adam.[14]

Malleus Maleficarum. Of all the references to Genesis 2, this one from medieval Christianity is the strangest. A manual to be used in tracking down witches, the book is filled with vicious stereotypes about women:

But the natural reason is that she is more carnal than a man, as is clear from her many carnal abominations. And it should be noted that there was a defect in the formation of the first woman, since she was formed from a bent rib. . . . It is clear in the case of the first women that she had little faith; for when the serpent asked why they did not eat of every tree in Paradise, she answered: of every tree, etc—lest perchance we die. Thereby she doubted, and had little faith in the word of God. And this is indicated by the etymology of the word; for *Femina* comes from *Fe* and *Minus*, since she is the weaker to hold and preserve the faith.[15]

Sirach. Jewish sources often show a more balanced interpretation of Genesis 2 and 3 than early Christian sources, even at times blaming Adam instead of Eve for disobedience.[16] But there are some that blame Eve, such as the apocryphal book Sirach from the second century BCE:

> From a woman sin had its beginning,
> And because of her we all die.[17]

Philo of Alexandria. In the first century of the Common Era, Philo combined for his interpretation of Genesis 2 and 3 a deep appreciation for Judaism with the Greek view that women in every way are weaker than men:

> Why does the serpent speak to the woman and not to the man? Woman is more accustomed to being deceived than man. For his judgment, like his body, is masculine and is capable of dissolving or destroying the designs of deception; but the judgment of woman is more feminine, and because of softness she easily gives way and is taken in by plausible falsehoods which resemble the truth.[18]

By today's standards, these interpretations of the Yahwist story seem extreme and unfair to what the Yahwist story actually says. Yet, many feminists would argue, we should recognize that the story does present the woman as secondary and plants the seeds that grow into these misogynist interpretations.[19]

ADAM, EVE, AND LILITH

Lilith has become a favorite among Jewish feminists who dislike the way the Yahwist story treats the woman. Who is Lilith? From legends told and retold in medieval Judaism, Lilith was described as Adam's first wife, a woman who did not work out the way God planned and Adam hoped, so she ended up being banished from the garden to make way for a subservient second wife, Eve.

The story of Lilith is an example of midrash, a Jewish tradition of asking questions of the Bible and then spinning out possible answers. Recognizing that one woman was created by God in Genesis 1 and another woman appears to have been created in Genesis 2, rabbis asked if this means Adam had two wives. And if so, what happened to the first? *The Alphabet of Ben Sira* (an anonymous work from the ninth or tenth century) calls the first wife Lilith and says she considered it demeaning to lie on the bottom when having sex, so a domestic quarrel resulted and she fled.[20] Legends grew to make Lilith a demon who endangered newborns, stalked men who slept alone, and gave birth to more demons who did all manner of harm.

Judith Plaskow in 1972 transformed Lilith from demon into feminist hero in her "The Coming of Lilith."[21] As Plaskow notes, this retelling is a midrash on a midrash and thus is part of the Jewish approach to the Bible.[22] In being a challenge to both Adam and to the male God who creates, it also is part of a Jewish tradition that allows humans to argue with God.

Here is a summary of Plaskow's retelling:

- God created Adam and Lilith from the dust of the ground and breathed into them the breath of life. They were equal, but since Adam was a man, he did not think Lilith equal and expected her to wait on him and to do most of the daily work in the garden. Lilith rebelled and ran away. Adam complained to God about "that uppity woman." It was then that God created a second and obedient woman from Adam's rib, Eve.
- Eve and Adam then lived happily, although Eve sometimes sensed undeveloped capacities in herself and was a little disturbed by the closeness between God and Adam. Adam, fearing the intrusion of Lilith in his paradise, built a wall around Eden to keep her out and told stories of the fearsome demon who had once lived with him.
- Lilith attempted to storm the garden's gate and failed, but it was then that Eve got a glimpse of the first woman and saw one very much like herself. Eve's curiosity grew, and one day she climbed a tree and swung over the wall. Lilith and Eve met and spent hours sharing each other's stories.
- For both God and Adam, things had not worked out according to plan. Plaskow's retelling ends with, "And God and Adam were expectant and afraid the day Eve and Lilith returned to the garden, bursting with possibilities, ready to rebuild it together."

In commenting on the fame that "The Coming of Lilith" has attained in the feminist community, Plaskow notes the centrality of sisterhood. A woman alone in a patriarchal religion is overwhelmed with male images and traditions. Christianity tends to focus on the individual and his or her relation with God, while Judaism thinks in terms of the collective experience of a people. Christian women too often stand lonely in their search for the very American goal of self-fulfillment, while Jewish feminists know more of collective experience and can more easily focus on sisterhood.[23] Lilith and Eve need each other, and only together may they stand strong.

DEFENDERS OF THE YAHWIST— TRIBLE AND BLOOM

In the face of widespread feminist rejection, the Yahwist account does find a vigorous defense from two scholars—a Christian feminist, Phyllis Trible, and a Jewish secularist, Harold Bloom.[24]

Phyllis Trible disagrees with most of her peers and argues that the Yahwist account is actually positive toward women. She says that we usually do not read Genesis 2 and 3 for what they actually say but are influenced by what males have said through the centuries. We must reread with unbiased eyes.[25]

- Man is *not* created first and woman last, as tradition has read it. Created first is *'adam*, whom Trible calls "earth creature." This earth creature is not male or female or an androgynous combination of the two.[26] After the garden is created with its creatures and vegetation, the last act of creation is the creation of human sexuality as male and female emerge simultaneously from the earth creature.
- The naming motif is not part of the creation story. "She shall be called woman" is a play on the words *ish* (man) and *ishshah* (woman) and is not a naming

but a description of the close relationship between the
two. Later, after the creation is complete and the pair
has disobeyed God, only then does the man name the
woman Eve.

- The woman is incorrectly pictured as man's helper
  in most translations, for the English word implies a
  secondary servant status. The Hebrew word translated
  "helper" is *ezer*, a word often used to refer to Yahweh
  as this God relates to the people Israel. If Yahweh is
  ezer, the word obviously cannot refer to one who is
  inferior. A better translation is "companion."
- Why does the serpent approach the woman first?
  Trible argues it is because the woman is the more
  interesting and intelligent of the pair. In making her
  the focus of the story, the storyteller focuses on the
  woman and her laudable traits. The man is "silent,
  passive, and bland" by comparison. The Yahwist
  is paying her a compliment, not blaming her for
  weakness.

Trible thus argues that the Yahwist may be seen as an ad-
mirer of the woman, if one reads with a fresh and nonpatriar-
chal approach. "Eve is theologian, ethicist, hermeneut, preacher,
and Rabbi. She defies the stereotype of patriarchal culture."[27]

Harold Bloom is neither a biblical scholar nor a specialist
in religion. He is a professor of comparative literature, one who
has spent decades studying the complexities of languages and
literary texts. Late in his career he developed his lifelong interest in the Yahwist into a 1990 best seller, *The Book of J.*[28] Bloom
argues that the original written text of the Yahwist account
was changed significantly by later editors, as they molded it

to serve their developing worship of Yahweh and as they attached it to the Priestly account. Digging into the Hebrew text of today's Genesis, Bloom thinks he can uncover the remnants of an earlier Yahwist text and learn much of its author's style and worldview. When we do this, we discover one of the great literary geniuses of all time, one equal to Shakespeare.[29]

And *surprise*. Bloom thinks the Yahwist was a woman. He theorizes that she was a great lady who worked in the court of King Solomon's inept son Rehoboam as the kingdom began to crumble. She was a friend of a court historian who wrote 2 Samuel and was brilliant with the Hebrew language, as may be seen in the careful choice of words and the several plays on words in the story. She is not herself a worshipper of Yahweh, but Bloom calls her Yahweh's protagonist, one who saw this god as a bungler who did not know how to sculpt a human figure and who needed human help in naming the animals. Bloom thinks for this female genius Yahweh was very different from the God of the biblical editors and writers to follow, and subsequently different from the God worshipped by Jews, Christians, and Muslims.[30]

Being a woman, the author makes the first woman central to the story, giving six times more space to the woman's creation than to the man's. She uses humor, and Bloom notes that when Yahweh forms the man from the ground, the picture is of a childish god playing to make man as a "mud pie." The woman, being more important, is not made from mud but from a living being. Women are strong and decisive, with men by comparison described as weak and childish. According to Bloom's reading, Moses in later chapters is a tormented weakling in the Yahwist telling.

The analyses of Phyllis Trible and Harold Bloom add original and interesting interpretations of the Yahwist story. Bloom's virtuoso interpretation may be admired, but few would line up to give it support.[31] Trible finds some supporters for her re-reading, but most feminists continue to read the story as hope-lessly biased against women.

THE PRIESTLY STORY—
PATRIARCHY AND HIERARCHY

In comparison with the Yahwist, the Priestly story for femi-nists seems to smell like roses. After all, man and woman are created at the same time ("male and female he created them"), and there is no hint of male superiority. Elizabeth Cady Stanton could be happy. But today's feminists say the Priestly story is more complicated than a cursory reading would indicate, and this story also falls under feminist suspicion. While the Yahwist goes into detail about the creation of the man and the woman, the Priestly account has a different theme; it is almost a creedal testimony to the great power and majesty of the cre-ator Elohim. Here we are into feminist theology.

A central concern in feminist critiques is *patriarchy*,[32] and the foundation stone for patriarchy is the image of God. God is commonly pictured in the Bible as a wise male who creates and rules and disciplines. Around this image the whole patriarchal society revolves—kings and tribal leaders and prophets and priests are males who are responsible to God, and in the fam-ily the husband is a patriarch to whom God delegates author-ity and responsibility. Patriarchy is manifest in the enormous emphasis on genealogies (through the male, of course) in the Hebrew Bible and New Testament.[33] The political, economic, educational, familial, and religious structures all are dominated by this image of a male God and those males in his image, with debilitating consequences for women.

"If God is male, then the male is God" is an oft-quoted dictum from post-Christian philosopher Mary Daly,[34] and it may be considered a battle cry for even moderate feminists. So, we must ask, is Elohim of the Priestly story a male? If answering from general Western culture, we must answer yes.

There is no better example of this male God than the masterpiece found on the ceiling of the Sistine Chapel in the Vatican, the section where Michelangelo interprets the Priestly story. The index finger of an older bearded man stretches out, almost touching the finger of the younger man. The picture cannot be referring to the Yahwist story, in which the first man is formed from dust, so it obviously is picturing the Priestly account in which 'adam is formed in the "image of God." But Michelangelo got it wrong. His painting does not reflect what Genesis 1

THE CREATION OF ADAM

The Priestly story says "male and female he created them," but Michelangelo made the first human in the image of a male God. Photo ©Erich Lessing/Art Resource, N.Y. Used by permission.

says, for the Priestly writer says clearly that first humanity was not a single male but "male and female." Where is the female in Michelangelo's picture? Michelangelo does a great injustice to women by reflecting the patriarchal bias of the West.

The great majority of Jews and Christians in the West have followed Michelangelo in imagining the God of Genesis as male. The image of an all-powerful and transcendent Elohim is easily open to patriarchal interpretations, as Christians have said in their creed, "I believe in God the Father Almighty, maker of heaven and earth."

Hierarchy is another big negative for feminists. Patriarchy and hierarchy go hand in hand, for both rest on presuppositions about how existence (and power) is organized. Even today many think hierarchically—of God and heaven above, of spirit above matter, of humans above nature. In the Priestly account God is pictured as existing before and above the world he creates, with humans in the image of this God and also above the created world. This hierarchical thinking is reflected in the New Testament, where Paul, in commenting on the Yahwist story, says that "Christ is the head of every man, and the husband is the head of his wife, and God is the head of Christ" (1 Cor 11:3). Hierarchy is also of major concern for environmentalists, as will be seen in the next chapter, for it makes the "other world" more important than this world and places both God and humans in positions of authority over the natural world. Environmental and feminist concerns join in ecofeminism.

Feminists often point out that the bias against women in the Bible is intensified when Christianity (and to a lesser degree, Judaism) is influenced by hierarchical Greek thought. Especially in the Platonic way of thinking, to penetrate behind the shadowy appearance of things and into the nature of existence is to discover a marvelous hierarchical world of higher realms.

The higher world includes God and spirit and heaven and the rational human soul, while the lower world is made up of material things, which have no ultimate value or permanence. The result is a dualism of spirit and matter. Women are creatures of the material world and have little capacity for insights concerning the higher world. This cosmic hierarchy of Greek thought is far removed from the earth-based perspective of the creation stories, but the Bible through its patriarchal ways of thinking also presupposes hierarchy and has contributed to an understanding of women as inferior.[35]

A song common among Christian youth at summer camps and church meetings in the past spoke of climbing "Jacob's ladder," of going higher and higher and being "soldiers of the cross." For feminist critics this represents hierarchy (climbing higher, higher) and patriarchy (Jacob, soldiers). As a substitute, using the same tune, "Sarah's Circle" is often sung, in which an inclusive circle gets "wider, wider" until it embraces "sisters, brothers, all."

GOD AS NEITHER MALE NOR FEMALE IN THE PRIESTLY STORY?

If, as we saw in our first chapter, the God of the Genesis stories does not create by sex, may we avoid a sexual bias by recognizing Elohim as neither male nor female? A quest for nongendered language about God presents problems that feminists are quick to point out. The most obvious is that the languages being dealt with (Hebrew, Greek, English) are languages in which nouns involve gender and in which pronouns present a thicket of challenges. The NRSV attempts to be gender inclusive, but the translators run into problems with the Hebrew—the language has only male and female genders (no neuter), and the names Elohim and Yahweh are both male in gender. It follows from this that the male pronoun is used, so the NRSV has no choice but to recognize God as "he" nine times in the Priestly story. The biblical understanding of God insists on personal anthropomorphic images, and our language knows only one way—if it is personal, it must be male or female. The Bible almost always chooses the male.

There is another problem with nongendered language. Western ideas about God are so tied to male images that even if gender-neutral language is used, the characteristics of God will still be what most people think of as male. Terms such as "Ground of Being" or "Absolute Other" may sound nongendered, but they easily mask patriarchal characteristics such as power and transcendence. And if the images are visual, as in Michelangelo's Sistine Chapel painting, God will be male.

Gender-neutral language thus does not draw full support among feminists. Are we stuck with male images, which so often become patriarchal and harmful to women? The solution of some feminists is to accept male images, reform these, and then balance them with female images.[36]

FEMALE IMAGES OF GOD
IN THE HEBREW BIBLE
(BUT NOT IN GENESIS)

In a search for female images, feminists start with the Bible. No doubt at one time in Israel female images were common, some argue, but these were blotted out or driven underground by the dominant patriarchy of the leaders of Israel and later of Christianity. Some do survive at a few places in the Hebrew Bible, and these show that patriarchy did not gain a total monopoly.

God is pictured as a woman carrying Israel in her womb and giving birth, in Isaiah (42:14; 46:3) and Deuteronomy (32:18). Isaiah further says God nurses her child (49:15) and comforts as a mother comforts her child (66:13). In Psalms (22:9) God is described as a midwife, and a number of times in several books God provides water and food—tasks that were assigned to women in the society of that day. One of the most significant images is found in the Hebrew words that are translated as "compassion" and "love," Hebrew terms that relate clearly to the Hebrew word for "womb."[37] Divine compassion evokes womb imagery, a God with deep maternal love for Israel. These are vivid female images of God with a womb and breasts.[38]

Further, Wisdom is pictured in Proverbs as a female persona of God in the creative process, an immanent presence of God in all things. Indeed, Proverbs 8, with its powerful female imagery of Wisdom, may be considered a creation story parallel to the two Genesis stories. Feminists who celebrate *sophia* (wisdom) as a female manifestation of the divine are drawing upon key biblical passages.[39]

If there were female images for God in the two Genesis creation stories, no doubt there would be enthusiasm for the stories from more feminists. Indeed, some have suggested amendments, such as Elizabeth Johnson's substitution for Genesis 1:2: "In the beginning she hovers like a great mother bird over her egg, to hatch the living order of the world out of primordial chaos."[40]

GOD AS MOTHER
(BEYOND THE BIBLE)

A host of feminist theologians have for a generation been engaged in assessing the religious and theological legacy of the Bible, and they have developed important and fruitful theologies to correct and enhance traditional theologies. For example, the image of God as Mother has been enthusiastically supported by some feminists and has been developed in considerable detail in the writings of theologian Sallie McFague. Here are points from McFague's argument:[41]

- It must be recognized that all talk about God is *metaphorical*. God is beyond the capacity of human beings to describe, so the best we can do is to stretch our imaginations and come up with images that do the best job of describing the indescribable. Metaphors for God paint pictures, they are fictions, they are symbols and not descriptions.[42] The idea of God as Mother is not saying God *is* mother, but it is saying that this is a most useful metaphor for God in our times.

- To think of God as Mother is not to abandon thinking of God as Father. God as Father can also be a useful metaphor, but unfortunately it is a good metaphor "gone astray" and become dominated by patriarchal, monarchical, and dualistic associations.[43] If we continue to think of God as Father, we must avoid traditional triumphalist images of power and transcendence that put this patriarchal Father above and beyond in a hierarchical dualism that separates God and world.[44]

- *Womb* is central in an understanding of God as Mother. McFague argues:

> There is simply no other imagery available to us that has the power of expressing the interdependence and interrelatedness of life with its ground. All of us, female and male, have the womb as our first home, all of us are born from the bodies of our mothers, all of us are fed by our mothers. What better imagery could there be for expressing the

most basic reality of existence: that we live and move and have our being in God?[45]

McFague's emphasis is on the symbols of *gestation, birth, and lactation* in the metaphor, very physical experiences that bond a child to its mother in a way very different from any bonding with a father. In the focus on mothering, she is avoiding ideas of the feminine with accompanying ideas of emotion and passivity, stereotypes that often do harm to women.[46]

- A focus on mother and womb supports the idea that the entire cosmos is the *body of God*. Male images for God, those closely associated with the Priestly creation story, have often been understood to involve preexistence and transcendence, which in turn have resulted in the dualistic idea that God is spirit and separate from the world of matter. To employ metaphors, when a male fathers, his creation is *apart from* his body, an image with major limitations. By comparison, when a female mothers, that which is created is *within* and then is "bodied forth" from her, a more appropriate image in an age with ecological sensitivity. Genesis 1 presents a male metaphor of the spirit of God moving over the face of the waters, a metaphor in which spirit is separate from matter. A female retelling of the story might see a womb in the midst of the waters, a female presence from which all life comes.[47] Along these lines, McFague is critical of the familiar Jewish and Christian teaching of creation out of nothing, for it allows God to exist before and apart from the world.[48]

To insist on maternal images of God means to introduce a

new way of thinking radically different from the Western patriarchal symbols usually associated with Genesis. McFague and some other feminists are not warm to either Genesis creation story, and it is understandable that they would like to develop alternatives. Both McFague and Ruether argue for a new story of creation, a story that comes out of modern scientific understandings of how the cosmos evolved and a story more compatible with the idea of God as Mother.[49] Judith Plaskow's retelling of the Lilith legend, noted earlier in this chapter, is another new story to replace the biblical stories of creation, as is the new story presented by ecologian Thomas Berry and discussed in the next chapter.

EVANGELICAL REACTIONS TO THE FEMINIST CHALLENGE

"Beware of the dangers of feminism" is a common message in the powerful and influential movement in which most call themselves "evangelicals" and many "evangelical fundamentalists." Yet there are some evangelical women who may be classed as feminists, and they have support from a number of men. These are Bible believers but usually not literalists, so it is better to identify them as evangelicals and not fundamentalists.[50] They reject the claim that much of the Bible is harmful toward women, and they are comfortable with the patriarchy of the Bible and the image of a Father God. Their argument is that *the problem is not with the Bible, which after all was revealed by God; the problem is that the Bible has been misinterpreted in ways that do harm to women.* Their position is advanced in an organization, Christians for Biblical Equality, that argues that woman and man were created for full and equal partnership with no implication whatsoever of female subordination.[51] This is the "egalitarian" position among evangelicals.

By contrast, another evangelical camp is "complementarian." This position is advanced by another organization, the Council for Biblical Manhood and Womanhood, which insists that men and women were created for different roles in family, church, and society. "Adam's headship in marriage was established by God," and the wife must follow her husband. Only men may be leaders and pastors in churches, with women supporting.[52]

Note that both organizations emphasize their *biblical* foundation. Each is reading the Genesis account carefully in an attempt to find its plain meaning. Here is a sample from their debate:

- Egalitarians say that Genesis 1:26-28 shows that both man and woman are in God's image and were created to share the responsibilities of bearing and rearing children, having dominion over the created order, and serving in church and society. Complementarians say that while Genesis 1 does describe the equal dignity of man and woman in the image of God, in Genesis 2 the man is created first and thus is given primacy and authority in the created order, a view emphasized in 1 Timothy 2:12. There has sadly been much abuse by husbands of their wives, but this does not remove God's intent that the husband should be the loving head of his family. Egalitarians respond that if being created first implies authority, then the animals would rule over humans, for they were created first in Genesis 1. They further say that when Genesis 3:16 says the man will rule over his wife, this is a description of conditions after sin entered the world, not the original intent of God.

- The statement that the woman was created as a helper for the man is central for the complementarians. "The woman was created to help her husband; her function is dependent on him. As she followed him in creation, she is to follow his lead as her husband."[53] Egalitarians, like Christian feminists generally, note that the Hebrew word translated "helper" (*ezer*) is used often to refer to God (clearly not a secondary being), and the woman should be understood as a partner to the man, an essential and equal counterpart.

- Further, complementarians note that God chooses to use the masculine noun *'adam* in Genesis 1:26 to represent all humanity, thus showing the primacy of the male,[54] an argument also used against inclusive language translations. Egalitarians respond that the message of scripture is from God, but the actual words are human, and since the text says that *'adam* is "male and female," it is very appropriate to translate "humankind" or "human beings."

The debate about Genesis between these camps of evangelicals goes on and on, point and counterpoint. Wayne Gruden of the Council for Biblical Manhood and Womanhood, for example, thinks the egalitarian view of Genesis has not been proven and that the controversy is essentially over. A benchmark was the 1998 adoption by the sixteen-million member Southern Baptist Convention of a complementarian statement that "a wife is to submit herself graciously to the servant leadership of her husband."[55] But the egalitarians have hardly thrown in the towel and now have an inclusive language translation of the favored New International Version of the Bible, as will be seen in appendix A. Through their books and organization, egalitarians are on a mission to change the evangelical movement.

How do these egalitarian evangelicals fit in the overall feminist picture? They may be considered a conservative wing of feminism, removed from those we have been considering and even farther from those who reject Judaism and Christianity outright. Many would not call themselves feminists, and their numbers and influence are not large. In contrast to these evangelicals, our focus in this chapter has been on the center of the movement, those reformist movers and shakers whose voices are being heard and who are making waves and having considerable influence in the mainstreams of Judaism and Christianity.

CONCLUSION

Feminists are not timid in their challenges, and most are not willing to accept halfway responses. For the Jewish and Christian feminists we have considered, the problems for women will not be solved by having female clergy in male-dominated institutions or by being awarded an equal place at the feet of a powerful Father God. Judaism and Christianity are so seeped in patriarchy, often in ways not recognized, that a top-to-bottom reexamination of all inherited ways of thinking and acting is needed.

It is understandable, then, that the Genesis creation stories should come under a shadow of suspicion. Except for Phyllis Trible's enthusiasm, the Yahwist account with its story of Adam, Eve, and the serpent does not sit well with feminists. The Priestly story fares little better, for the God of "in the beginning" seems very much like a male power figure. The creation stories thus are not likely to be found in those selections from the Bible that most feminists find helpful or even inspirational.

We must be sympathetic to feminist ideas and recognize that patriarchy and hierarchy are major problems that must be addressed when reading the Bible. Having said this, however, it is possible to have more respect for the creation stories than is found in most feminist discussions. In the creation stories and in Jewish and Christian feminist discussions, a major focus is upon how God is to be understood. We have argued that God in the creation stories is not male, in spite of our male-biased languages and our common way of thinking. The understanding of God in Genesis is open equally to female and male symbolic language, and we should think of the Creator as both Mother and Father as we interpret the two stories.

CHAPTER 3

GENESIS AND THE CRITIQUES OF ENVIRONMENTALISTS

For humans to cause species to become extinct . . . for humans to degrade the integrity of Earth by causing changes in its climate, by stripping the Earth of its natural forests . . . for humans to contaminate the Earth's waters, its land, its air, and its life . . . these are sins.

—ECUMENICAL PATRIARCH
BARTHOLOMEW[1]

THE CREATION STORIES in Genesis have contributed to the catastrophic deterioration of our natural world. Such was the claim in a blockbuster article published in 1967 in the scholarly journal *Science*, an article reprinted in numerous places and precipitating a heated debate. This claim about Genesis is a focus in a new cutting-edge field in religious studies and in theology, a field dealing with religion and the natural world.

The article was by the medieval historian Lynn White Jr.[2] In it he argued that "Christianity bears a huge burden of guilt" for the ecological crisis, and he came down hard on the Genesis stories, faulting both accounts for putting humans in charge. For Genesis, White argued, "no item in the physical creation had any purpose save to serve man's purposes." The stories set the stage for the view that the earth is raw material to be used in any way that humans wish. White was sharp in his criticism:

> Especially in its Western form, Christianity is the most anthropocentric religion that the world has seen. . . . Man shares, in great measure, God's transcendence of nature. Christianity, in absolute contrast to ancient paganism and Asia's religions . . . not only established a dualism of man and nature but also insisted that it is God's will that man exploit nature for his proper ends.

Some Jewish and Christian scholars side with White in his criticism of the Genesis stories.[3] Others vigorously defend the stories and argue that White and other critics get it all wrong, do not understand the biblical accounts, and have not done adequate research on how they have been understood through the centuries. So here is the debate.

BLAMING GENESIS

The criticism starts with the Priestly account, in which humans are created last, as the pinnacle of creation. God then says:

> "Be fruitful and multiply, and fill the earth and subdue it; and have dominion over the fish of the sea and over the birds of the air and over every living thing that moves upon the earth." (Gen 1:28)

The expressions "have dominion" (*rada* in Hebrew) and "subdue" (*kabash*) are lightning rods for much of the discussion. *Rada* refers to the absolute power of rulers in the ancient world and includes the enslavement of conquered peoples. *Kabash* could also be translated "tread upon," for it refers to stomping grapes when making wine and, by inference, to what victors were expected to do with a defeated enemy. The terms indeed are harsh, and the Priestly storyteller presupposes humanity will flourish only when humans exert control.[4]

This "dominate and subdue" approach, according to critics, has become the common view in most endeavors of the modern world. With encouragement from Genesis, modern science and commerce have pushed humans to exploit their world in increasingly damaging ways. The prevailing attitude is "If it grows, cut it down; if it moves shoot it."[5] Or, as early scientist Francis Bacon thought, nature is an anvil on which humans hammer out a world. This view is still on occasion found in official Christian statements, as when Pope John Paul II in 1995 said, "Everything in creation is ordered to man and everything is made subject to him."[6] It is found in a "Dear Abby" column in which a women wrote in that she wears a fur coat because "the Bible gave man dominion over animals."[7]

This dominion theme is augmented by the notion of humans bearing an "image of God." The Priestly account says, "So God created humankind in his image, in the image of God he created them." Here only humans bear God's image, no other creatures. The image of God has been a popular theme for interpretation through the centuries and is often seen as implying that humans are like God in many ways—including the ability to speak, the capacity to make covenants, and the responsibility and accountability that go with mature rationality. According to the Priestly storyteller, although the waters and the earth "brought forth," they did not bring forth humans. Humans are of God's direct making, created by the power of the divine voice, created to be like God. If God, humans, and the world are the three major components of existence, then being created in God's image implies that God and humans are close partners, both transcending and ruling over the world. Because humans are in the image of God, there are both *closeness* between God and humans and *distance* between humans and a natural world that lacks God's image. President George W. Bush reflected the Priestly account in saying, "Humans are not animals. We did not come from nor belong to this earth. We are created by God to have superiority over all life on earth."[8]

Turning to the older Yahwist story, we do not find language like "dominion" or "image of God." Yet, using a very different style, the Yahwist also emphasizes the centrality of humanity, in this case male humanity. As we have seen from feminist concerns, the Yahwist has the man being created first, followed by a garden that is created for the man and finally by a woman who is created to be man's helper. In this traditional reading of the Yahwist account, the man is primary.

There is also for the Yahwist a theme similar to dominion in the Priestly account. The storyteller says the LORD God brought animals and birds to the man to see what he would call them. "And whatever the man called every living creature, that was its name" (Gen 2:19). Our use of names today is rather utilitarian, and we often consider names as no more than useful handles. But that was not the case for many ancient peoples. A name often involved power, so great care was exercised in applying a name, including the name for God. Thus man assumes power in giving names to all living creatures and somewhat later to his wife. Naming is similar to dominion.

Both stories describe a basic *distance* between humans and other creatures and recognize a special status for humans. Critics argue that, by comparison, the creation stories of a number of other peoples offer a wise focus on the *closeness* between humans and the natural world. North American Indians, for example, say that humans need to learn from their relatives the buffalo and eagle and salmon. Further, the earth is spoken of as Mother—with rocks described as Mother's bones, mountains as breasts, grass as hair, caves as wombs—and humans must avoid harm to their mother.[9] By comparison, the Genesis stories establish a foundation for human arrogance and abuse of the natural world.

IN DEFENSE OF GENESIS

These criticisms of Genesis have elicited vigorous and detailed responses. *Genesis must be defended, not blamed or abandoned*, argue many Jewish and Christian scholars. Critics have it all wrong because both the Priestly and Yahwist storytellers present positive views of the natural world and can be dynamic resources in addressing the ecological crisis.

The creation stories reflect a covenant involving God, nature, and humans. They must never be understood apart from the active role of this creator God. Covenant is usually understood as a theme in the exodus from Egypt when God and the Israelites established a special relationship, a covenant involving God's actions in history. But covenant is also in Genesis, a covenant involving the natural world. "God blessed them" and in turn clear covenantal responsibilities were established for humans.[10] This is no absentee deist God but one actively involved in nature as well as history and who holds humans accountable.

Humans are closely tied to the natural world in the Genesis stories, and the critics are not correct in seeing a distance between humans and the rest of creation. Note the language in the Yahwist account. The LORD God "formed man from the dust of the ground," a theme picked up a little later in a passage cited in funerals today, "You are dust, and to dust you shall return" (2:7 and 3:19). There is a play on words in the Hebrew text where *'adam* comes from *'adama,* usually translated "man from the dust of the ground." Translations often miss this play on words, so alternates have been suggested for *'adam* from *'adama*—"earth creature from the earth,"[11] "human from the humus,"[12] "the groundling from the ground."[13] Humans are made from the ground, they walk on it and cultivate it while they live, and they return to it in death.

This "groundling from the ground" in the Yahwist account comes from a farming community and reflects a traditional close bond of farmers with their land and their domesticated animals. According to the Yahwist, *'adam* is created to serve the *'adama* to help the ground be fertile and productive. The story starts with both the LORD God and the man caring for the ground, the LORD God sending rain and the man tilling the ground.

Yet, according to the Yahwist, *'adam* is more than a "groundling from the ground," for the LORD God "breathed into his nostrils the breath of life; and the man became a living being"(2:7). The Hebrew word *nephesh* is translated here "living being" and sometimes translated "living soul." This is clearly not the "soul" of Greek thought but that vital essence that makes one live. Humans have it, but animals also have it throughout the Hebrew Bible. Not just in being a groundling but also in becoming a living being like the animals, humans are part of the natural order for the Yahwist.[14]

May we say the same about the Priestly account? There is an interesting twist in the Priestly telling, and we owe it to

Jewish scholars to pick this up. God said to the humans, "Be fruitful and multiply," a natural function that humans share with other animals. Thus humans *are* part of the natural order, as they are for the Yahwist. But the Priestly author also has God say "subdue" and "have dominion," representing a higher status that relates to the image of God and not to the natural order. In saying "have dominion," the Priestly account adds a paradoxical responsibility, a like-God quality for humans, who clearly are rooted in the natural order by the command "Be fruitful and multiply."[15]

Land is a clear focus in both accounts. Land has been a major theme in Jewish thought, with much of Jewish history focusing on the ancient and modern experience of living in a special land in the Near East, and on promises and diasporas and exiles in which Jews have dreamed of this land. A Hebrew word usually translated "land" is *eretz*, which implies a broader expanse than *'adama* and often refers to a specific geographical area. The sense of an earthly place central to the two creation stories has contributed to a mind-set that has kept Judaism rooted to life in this world.[16]

Land is less important in Christianity than in Judaism, but there is a growing interest in land among Christians. Land helps to offset a tendency to focus too much on a heavenly world while abandoning the natural world. Biblical scholar Walter Brueggemann argues in *The Land* that land is a "prism for biblical faith," with the focus in the Bible beginning with "actual earthly turf" and continuing into a promise in which land symbolizes hope and deliverance.[17] There is also considerable support in Christian circles for the land ethic of Aldo Leopold, an ecologist from the early twentieth century who argued that land is a biotic community where humans and other creatures hold citizenship.[18]

Limits upon human activity are set clearly by the Genesis stories and how they have been interpreted. Much has been made of "have dominion" and "subdue" by critics who argue that Genesis gives humans control over the natural world. Taken out of context, this might be an acceptable interpretation, but Jews and Christians have often recognized that within the covenant with God there is both a special standing for the created order and clear restraints.[19] Here are examples of these limits on human activity.

Vegetarianism. The Priestly account pictures a world so irenic and nonviolent that both humans and other creatures are limited in what they eat. Fruit and seeds and green plants are given for food, and there is no killing in God's creation. Most who read the story miss the point that the original humans were vegetarians, and meat-eating (again, within limits) was not accepted until Noah's time.[20] There are today Jewish and Christian organizations promoting vegetarianism as an article of faith, both arguing that Genesis states that it was God's original intent for all to be vegetarians.[21]

The Sabbath. The clearest limits on human activity are connected to the Priestly account's seventh day. The Sabbath involves rest for humans but also a weekly rest for the land and all who live on the land. To supplement the weekly day of rest, Leviticus prescribes a sabbatical year for the land, where every seven years there is no plowing, sowing, pruning, or gathering: "It shall be a year of complete rest for the land."[22] The fact that most Jews and Christians today either ignore or severely water down sabbatical restrictions on human activity does not remove the biblical intent.

Bal Tashcit. This famous Jewish principle, "Do not destroy," has generated extensive rabbinic commentary for centuries. The reference is to Deuteronomy 20:19, where rules of war are set and God says that in a siege of a city "you must not destroy [*bal tashcit*] its trees." The background is respect for God's creation, and this clear limit on human activity by extension prohibits the heedless destruction of anything in nature.[23] The principle is central for Jewish environmental concerns and has informed the action of the "redwood rabbis" who have opposed the cutting of old-growth redwoods by Jewish businessmen in the lumber business in northern California.[24]

DISAGREEMENTS ABOUT STEWARDSHIP

Those who defend the Genesis stories usually emphasize stewardship. Humans do not own the earth but are "tenants" or "steward managers" of a beneficent world that ultimately belongs to God. Dominion in the Priestly story should be understood as stewardship, in which humans care for and serve the natural world.[25] In the words of the eighteenth-century Quaker William Penn, "We have nothing that we can call our own; no, not our selves: For we are all but Tenants, and at Will, too, of the great Lord of our selves, and the rest of this great Farm, the World that we live upon."[26]

Stewardship is the English word used in the translation of several passages in the Greek New Testament, and the original Greek helps in understanding its meaning. The word regularly translated "steward" is *oikonomos,* with *oikonomia* becoming "stewardship." *Oikos* means "household"—it is the root of the words *ecology, ecumenical,* and *economics. Nomos* means "to put in order." Thus the original meaning of our word *stewardship* refers to the action of a servant who supervises the domestic affairs of a household on behalf of a master, such as a lord or king. Everything in the created world is God's household, and humans are the servants who keep things in good order.[27]

Protestant and Catholic churches produce seemingly endless studies and statements, including significant pronouncements about how Christians should approach the environmental crisis. These all have a major emphasis on Christian stewardship. There are also Christian groups alongside the churches that focus on ecology, and these draw heavily upon Christian stewardship. A number of Christian scholars emphasize stewardship, especially Douglas John Hall, whose enthusiastic writings on stewardship have been widely read. For Judaism, both individual Jewish scholars and the Coalition on the Environment and Jewish Life place major emphasis on stewardship.[28] The list could go on.

Not all, however, are enthusiastic about stewardship. As a theme it has become shopworn or even distasteful in the experience of many Jews and Christians. Stewardship has lost its larger meaning, and for most people it refers to those self-serving annual campaigns by religious organizations to raise money for buildings and programs.[29] Add to this the fact that major corporations such as ExxonMobil, which by Jewish or Christian standards are poor stewards of the earth's bounty, actually advertise that they are good stewards.

The problem with stewardship, however, goes beyond its misuse. Critics say stewardship is based on an outdated anthropocentric view that the world was created for humans. It draws from the domination theme in Genesis and presupposes a hierarchical human superiority over nature. John Hart diagrams this as "God > humans > nature" and then says:

> In the hierarchy, humans are closer to God and serve as a bridge between God and nature. Humans mediate God to nature; nature does not mediate God to humans . . . such human hubris can inhibit human interrelatedness with creation. Members of stewardship traditions might not explore the depths of their connectedness to all creation.[30]

Those like Hart who are critical of stewardship say it should be used only with a recognition of the problems involved with the idea. Some go further and argue that we should retire "dominion" and "stewardship" as terms with too much harmful anthropocentric baggage.[31]

This debate about stewardship echoes the larger disagreement about the creation stories and reflects the dilemma many Jews and Christians face as they look at the environmental crisis. Does the tradition based on Genesis present a problem or a solution? This dilemma has led some to suggest new ways of thinking.

THE GREENING OF JEWISH AND CHRISTIAN THOUGHT

Traditionally Christians and Jews have focused on the relationship of God and humans. The result has been a kind of ellipse in thinking, with attention going back and forth between God and humans. Nature, if considered at all, was thought of as relatively unimportant or even as a temporary backdrop.

This was true of much of biblical scholarship in the twentieth century, which read the Hebrew scriptures as telling of the special relationship between a people and their God, a relationship that was concerned with human redemption through culture and history. At best, the natural world was considered a stage upon which the more important drama of redemption was acted out; at worst, it posed a threat because it represented those false gods and practices that biblical leaders were fighting against. In biblical scholarship this view of nature is "one of the reigning orthodoxies of our age," notes Theodore Hiebert, and it has dominated interpretations of the two creation stories.[32]

This approach to nature could also be found in the theologies that swept across the religious landscape. First, there was liberalism with its confidence in human ability and its optimism about progress, putting humanity's genius above the natural world. Next came neoorthodoxy, which spoke of human sin and limits and addressed the desperate conditions of world wars and cold wars, of holocaust and mass injustice. neoorthodoxy brought renewed focus on the Bible and on divine revelation as the proper source of insight in troubled times, while criticizing any natural theology that might find insight from the natural world. Then there was early liberation theology in its three forms—black theology, third-world theologies, feminist theology—which focused on class struggle and on the aspirations of oppressed peoples. These ways of thinking paid little attention to the natural world because attention was on how humans relate to God and to each other.[33]

There has now been a dramatic shift in the thinking of many, a greening in much of Jewish and Christian thought. *A major paradigm shift has replaced the ellipse of God and humans with a triangle of God, humans, and nature.* The natural world becomes a major focus—the ecocentric balances the anthropocentric and the theocentric.[34]

This shift from ellipse to triangle may be illustrated in the treatment of both sin and love, especially in Christian circles. Love, through seemingly endless sermons and books, has been thought of as a reflection of the two great commandments that Jesus chooses from the Hebrew Bible—love God and love neighbor. The absence of a love for nature is conspicuous, and now some are making the ellipse into a triangle—love God, love neighbor, love nature.[35] Likewise, sin has been thought of as against God or against neighbor, but now, as seen in the opening quote from Orthodox Patriarch Bartholomew, some are speaking of sins against nature. Contaminating the earth should be considered a sin alongside adultery and blasphemy.

A greening of Christian thought has even begun to be seen in some evangelical circles, where there has been general hostility toward relating Christianity to environmental concerns. The lively Evangelical Environmental Network, while promoting hybrid cars, transformed the traditional WWJD from meaning "What would Jesus *do*?" to "What would Jesus *drive*?" And in 2006 there was a major statement calling for legislation to combat global warming signed by eighty-six prominent evangelical leaders. Richard Cizik of the powerful National Association of Evangelicals has become a leader in these concerns, and the evangelical periodical *Christianity Today* has become outspoken.[36] Many evangelicals still oppose this new emphasis on the environment, but it is gaining support in a number of congregations.

PANENTHEISM AS GREEN THEOLOGY

Some venturesome green thinkers are now championing an increasingly influential theology known as *panentheism*.[37] This theology argues that classical theism, which has been so dominant in the West, has an inappropriate view of the natural world and must be changed. Classical theism is familiar:

- God created the world we live in, while existing before and apart from the world. God is transcendent or other.
- While apart from the world, God still cares for the world, sustains the world, is known in the world, and sometimes acts in special ways in the world. Thus at times God is immanent.
- God is personal. God is thought of anthropomorphically, having characteristics such as the ability to love, listen, and make choices.

- There is only one God, who is unchanging, absolute,
  all-powerful, and eternal. The created world is very
  different—it is finite and one day will end.

For some, this classical theism describes a God too separated
from the natural world, with the world understood as spun off
from God and existing at a secondary level. The not-God world
is of lower importance than God and the religious things involving God. This separation of God and natural world relates
to a number of harmful dualistic categories—heaven/earth,
spiritual/physical, soul/body, life eternal/life on earth. This
dualistic way of thinking devalues the natural world and leaves
the door open for major ecological trouble.

As a substitute for classical theism, panentheism is proposed. The term comes from the Greek: *pan* (all) *en* (in) *theos*
(God). All is in God, but God is more than all. Panentheism
is not to be confused with pantheism, where all (*pan*) is God
(*theos*) and God is all. A number of prominent thinkers now call
themselves panentheists. While noting that not all agree on all
points, we may identify some common themes:[38]

- It is appropriate to think of the natural world as the
  body of God. Feminists and nonfeminists alike make
  this point.
- The relationship between God and world is, by
  analogy, similar to how humans think their minds
  relate to their bodies. A person cannot think apart
  from a body, but mental activity is more than body.
  Likewise, God and world are intimately related; God is
  embodied, but God is more than the natural world.[39]
- God shares characteristics of the dynamic and
  evolving universe. Nothing is fixed, static, changeless,
  not even God. Gone are abstract ideas of pure essence

or absolute being in describing God. Insights from contemporary science are useful here, as they are throughout panentheistic thought.

- God and all parts of the universe are understood as a continuously interacting and interpenetrating cosmic community. All is related to all else, just as all relates to God and God to all.[40]
- God is not thought of in terms of power but in terms of support, as God humbly allows the cosmic community to develop in its own way.

Because panentheism is remarkably different from classical theism, it may seem new and strange. Advocates, however, argue that the overemphasis on transcendence in classical theism developed under the influence of Greek and medieval philosophy, after the Bible was complete. Often in the Bible God is seen intimately involved in the world, as St. Paul in the New Testament speaks of God "in whom we live and move and have our being."[41] Indeed, some argue that panentheism is more compatible with the Bible than is classical theism.[42]

FOR SOME CHRISTIANS, A SACRAMENTAL UNIVERSE

It follows from what has been said about panentheism that many Christians view the universe sacramentally. In churchly Christianity those rites known as sacraments are based on the premise that physical things are capable of hosting the sacred, a corollary of the belief that God became embodied in Jesus the Christ. Thus the bread and wine of the Eucharist become vehicles for the special presence of the Lord Jesus Christ, and Martin Luther could speak of Christ present "in, with, and under" the bread and wine. Arthur Peacocke draws a parallel and notes that "in, with, and under" is panentheistic language, describing a God who is present in all that exists.[43]

This emphasis upon the presence of God through Christ in all that exists has been common in Eastern Christianity. Orthodox theologian Kallistos Ware, readily calling himself a panentheist, writes, "If the doctrine of creation is to mean anything at all, it must signify that God is on the inside of everything, not on the outside. Creation is not something upon which God acts from the exterior, but something through which he expresses himself from within. Our primary image should be that of *indwelling*."[44] This indwelling in Eastern Christianity is often spoken of in terms of the *energy* of God that permeates all of creation, compared to a common Western idea of a God who in his pure being transcends creation.[45]

A common icon in Eastern Christianity is the Pantocrator, an image of Christ as the Lord of all that exists. A similar expanded view of Christ is gaining importance among environmentally sensitive Christians in the West who say that Jesus in his resurrection broke the bonds of finitude in becoming the Christ and is now present in the entire universe. He is a cosmic Christ. The New Testament letter to the Colossians proclaims that "all things in heaven and on earth" were created in Christ and "in him all things hold together." Indeed, Colossians six times connects the risen Christ to "all things."[46] For those who think in terms of a sacramental universe, what happens at the Lord's table is a reflection of a much larger drama, for the risen Christ is embodied not just in the bread and wine but in the entire universe.

Teilhard de Chardin's "Mass on the World" described conducting daily mass on the open steppes of Asia, but without bread and wine. With the whole earth as his altar, Teilhard called upon the rising sun to place on his paten the harvest of the earth's labors and to pour into his chalice sap from the earth's fruits.[47] Teilhard was consciously taking the sacramental ritual from the confines of church and into a cosmic realm.

Teilhard's mass was penned in 1923, and a recent example of his outlook is Matthew Fox's "Planetary Mass." Here is a multimedia experience with projections of DNA codes, dancing planets and galaxies and atoms, a sun altar and a moon altar, and a balance of male and female symbols. Using much that we have learned from science and from other cultures, the mass seeks to see the incarnation of the cosmic Christ through contemporary eyes.[48]

A panentheistic view and a sacramental view go hand in hand, for both insist that from the bread and wine of the Eucharist to the ground under our feet to the far reaches of the universe, all is infused with the presence of the sacred.

ECOFEMINISM

The problems women face all around the globe are linked directly with the crisis in the natural environment, according to feminists. It is not just coincidence that a common metaphor for human devastation of nature—"rape of the earth"—comes from the real experience of women. As Rosemary Radford Ruether says, "We cannot criticize the hierarchy of male over female without ultimately criticizing and overcoming the hierarchy of human over nature."[49] Classical theism with its male-like God presents a patriarchal model of domination that encourages males to rule over both women and the natural world. And the hierarchical outlook based on a heaven/earth dualism leaves both women and nature low in value. It follows that some feminists are enthusiastic panentheists.

Among ecofeminists there is considerable interest in the Gaia hypothesis developed by biologist James Lovelock. Gaia is a name ancient Greeks used for the earth, personified as a living goddess, a great mother. Lovelock has argued that we should think of the earth as Gaia, a superorganism that is more than a combination of all living earthly things. Gaia may be spoken of symbolically as a "she" who lives and is self-regulatory.[50] Rosemary Radford Ruether, using the Gaia hypothesis, says the voice of our mother the earth has long been silenced by our patriarchal God. Women and men must become sensitive anew to the voice of Gaia.[51]

Further, ecofeminism includes a major concern for justice. For many feminists, environmental concerns are as much about the plight of poor women as about the destruction of the natural world. Around the earth, it is women who feel the most immediate impact of environmental degradation, for it is women more than men who must day in and day out live with polluted water, with foul air, with industrial wastes, with poisoned infants, with systems that separate families from the land and imprison them in urban slums. Ivone Gebara ties her "urban ecofeminism" directly to the condition of women in her native Brazil. A Roman Catholic nun and teacher, she chooses to live with the poor and formulates her Christianity through the eyes of poor women.[52] Many feminists like Gebara are aware that sisterhood can too easily focus on middle-class women and that the masses of poor women must be of constant concern.

BEYOND GENESIS, A NEW STORY

In one generation we have come to know the universe as no humans before. The first landing on the moon in 1969 will always be noted as a benchmark in natural and human history. Soon afterward, millions of Americans sat before their televisions as Carl Sagan for thirteen weeks explored the universe and its history of billions of years. Then the Hubble telescope and its spectacular pictures began to inspire awe and fascination. The

Big Bang moved from a rather strange theory to the centerpiece of astrophysics. We have pushed our envelope of understanding with such measurements as a light-year, which is an almost inconceivable distance of six trillion miles, only to be told that some objects in our universe are billions of light-years away and that our universe is not the only one, for there may be billions of universes. We have come increasingly to realize that our universe home is fantastically old and incomprehensibly large; it is filled with mind-boggling energy and interrelationships.

Increasingly we have come to understand ourselves as cosmic citizens traveling on spaceship earth. The magnificent picture of our earth home, taken from a NASA spacecraft, has become a kind of religious icon, taking its place beside the Christian cross, the Jewish star of David, the Islamic crescent, and the Buddhist wheel of Dharma. Through high school and college science textbooks—as well as through popular avenues such as the National Geographic Society, the Smithsonian, the Hayden Planetarium, and the TV program *Nova*—a new story of the universe is being told. Unlike the Genesis stories and the many other creation stories from around the globe, this new story is truly universal and is becoming the common story of origins for all humanity.

A few voices call for giving up on the Genesis accounts because they are both out of date and harmful. Genesis should be replaced by this new story based upon the fantastic findings of science, they argue. Here a "geologian" tells the new story as an alternative to Genesis:

> In a great flash, the universe flared forth into being. In each drop of existence a primordial energy blazed with an intensity never to be equaled again. Thick with its power, the universe billowed out in every direction so that the elementary particles could stabilize, enabling the

AN ICON FOR A NEW CREATION STORY

The Andromeda Galaxy is, as NASA says, "a disk-like city of a trillion stars." The nearest neighbor to our own Milky Way, it is over two million light-years away. The bright center in the picture reflects the intense heat of cosmic dust, and astronomers point out numerous regions in Andromeda where stars are being born or are dying. Photo courtesy Jason Ware, www. galaxyphoto.com.

first atomic beings of hydrogen and helium to emerge. After a million turbulent years, the frenzied particles calmed themselves enough for the primeval fireball to dissolve into a great scattering, with all the atoms soaring away from each other into the dark cosmic skies opening up in the beginning of time.[53]

Thomas Berry is the coauthor of this quote and a leader in the call for a new story. He says the old Genesis stories now are dysfunctional.[54] We live between stories, for the new story is just unfolding and we are slowly learning to tell it. He argues that a radical reassessment of the human situation is needed and, as always has been the case, humans need a creation story of "how things came to be, how they came to be as they are, and how the future can be given some satisfying direction." Berry is a Roman Catholic priest, and clearly he is not arguing that science will take the place of religion and that scientists are the new prophets. He thinks the former hostility between science and religion has faded and that now scientists and religious thinkers, avoiding anthropocentrism, must work together in developing a new biocentric vision of humanity's role in the universe and a new commitment to the values that should guide the human journey.[55]

IN THE BEGINNING
AND IN THE ENDING

Before concluding this chapter, let us take a look at how visions of the future relate to the environmental crisis. Genesis tells how it all started "in the beginning," and the traditions that start with Genesis have added views of some future time "in the ending." This involves eschatology, meaning the last things in some future time or event. Life after death and its association with salvation are an eschatological hope for many, and this hope has direct implications for one's view of the natural world. Most Christians, along with a significant number of Jews, would say, "When I die, my soul will leave my body and I will live with God in heaven," not recognizing that such a statement may be earth-denying and ecologically harmful.

In a search for a more nature-positive and universe-affirming eschatology, the views of theologian Karl Rahner stand out. Rahner notes that most Christian views of life after death are dualistic—heaven and earth are separate realities and this creation will be abandoned for a more glorious *acosmic* heaven beyond this world. Rahner would like to avoid *acosmic* (not this cosmos) views and to think of life after death in *pancosmic* (all the cosmos) terms, envisioning an afterlife as not beyond the cosmos but within. As a Roman Catholic, Rahner continues to talk of a human soul but blunts any dualistic implication by calling it a "spiritual life-principle" that must always involve a body. The human soul during this life is related to one particular bit of the world, namely a human body. At death the soul is released from the limitations of one body and becomes embodied in the universe as a whole; it becomes *pancosmic*.[56] Rahner's view takes seriously both earth and cosmos as human homes.

Some who think of a life after death think also in terms of an apocalypse, a dramatic and sudden end to earthly life as we know it. Apocalyptic thinking is seldom found today in most of Judaism and Christianity, but it has received great emphasis in parts of the New Christian Right. Hal Lindsey's *The Late Great Planet Earth*, with its story of an upcoming cosmic disaster and the joyous "rapture" of true Christians, has convinced many. The Left Behind books by Tim LaHaye and Jerry Jenkins, a series that has sold sixty million copies, culminate in a final apocalypse where the earth is destroyed. Occasionally a public official such as Secretary of the Interior James Watt will say he is not concerned with ecological problems because the world will come to an end soon.[57] Anyone reexamining Jewish or Christian thought must recognize that apocalyptic views may be extremely harmful to any healthy concern for the natural world. The Genesis creation stories describe a natural world that is good and in which humans may expect a meaningful future, a view at odds with much of apocalypticism.

Eschatology is a complex area that is an essential part of both Judaism and Christianity. Themes such as the coming of the Messiah, the kingdom of God, the eternal soul, and resurrection of the body fit easily into the ellipse of God and humans and seldom are brought up when thinking about the natural world. Now green thinkers wisely want to replace the ellipse with a triangle and to insist that the natural world must be considered in every aspect of Jewish and Christian thought. Part of this must be a thorough reexamination of all aspects of eschatology.

CONCLUSION

A group of scientists meeting in Moscow in 1990 issued a strong statement that talked of the mounting "crimes against creation." Signed by leading scientists—including such familiar names as Steven Jay Gould and Carl Sagan—the statement was a call to leaders of all the great religions to help change human thought and behavior "because what is regarded as sacred is more likely to be treated with care and respect."[58] Recognizing that religions have a powerful influence on public opinion, the scientists joined many others who say the ecological crisis will not be met without the positive involvement of religion.

Increasing numbers of Jews and Christians agree and have begun to reexamine their approach to the natural world, an approach that is based on the creation stories in Genesis.

Before Judaism and Christianity can become part of the solution, it must first be admitted that they in some ways have been part of the problem. The debate precipitated by Lynn White's famous essay should lead to this confession. At the same time, blame should not be heaped on the creation stories, as was done by White. The stories no doubt have been interpreted in ecologically harmful ways, but defenders of the stories are correct in saying they have too often been interpreted incorrectly. The stories should not be blamed but should be seen as a resource in telling of human relationships with the natural world.

Understanding God is central to the interpretive task, as we saw in considering feminist views. A God radically apart from and different from creation—a common view of the God of Genesis 1—opens a path for seeing a cosmos devoid of any sense of the sacred and an earth open to exploitation. A different view and one better suited to our ecologically sensitive age is that of panentheism and its insistence that God is in all that exists, even that the cosmos is the body of God. Panentheism is found in much of the Bible and can be important in understanding the creation stories.

The call for new creation stories should also be welcomed. The stories in Genesis may be augmented without being abandoned. Stories of the origins of the universe coming from science paint a *cosmocentric* picture exceedingly moving and powerful. Stories from many native people such as the American Indians paint an *ecocentric* picture helpful in affirming the interrelationships of all living beings. Alternate stories with their difference of emphasis may be important supplements to the Genesis stories, where an *anthropocentric* drama tells of the relationship of humans to their creator and their world.

CHAPTER 4

GENESIS AND THE CLAIMS OF CREATIONISTS

Man in his arrogance thinks himself a great work,
worthy of the interposition of a deity.
— CHARLES DARWIN[1]

EACH YEAR in the heat of July, the people of Dayton, Tennessee, turn out for a reenactment of the 1925 Scopes "monkey trial." The old courthouse has been restored, and there the famous confrontation between Clarence Darrow and William Jennings Bryan may be witnessed anew. Afterward, a tour leads to twenty-seven sites related to the trial.

On a hill overlooking the town sits Bryan College, dedicated to the great fundamentalist and to the stand he took for the Bible and against false scientific views. Bryan College is a Christian college in a fundamentalist mold, where students study "biological origins from a biblical perspective." It has a Center for Origins Research, which supports the "creation model" of life's beginnings. The center publishes books used in Christian schools and maintains a Creation anti-Evolution Literature Database that has 18,000 entries. It also does research, especially in a field called baraminology, a term based on the Hebrew word *bara* in Genesis 1, which is "kind" in English translations.[2]

With Dayton and Bryan College, we are introduced to creationism. The term was coined in 1868 to emphasize the Genesis story of creation in opposition to evolution and Charles Darwin's ideas.[3] It was not until the 1960s, however, that the term came into common use and became identified with Young Earth Creationism—the view that includes a literal reading of Genesis, an age for the universe of less than 10,000 years, and a militant argument that Darwinian science must be replaced by creation science. Creationism and the spirit of Bryan are today found not just in a Bible Belt town but in all parts of the nation.

BACKGROUND:
FROM ARCHBISHOP USSHER
TO THE *SCOFIELD REFERENCE BIBLE*

Many growing up Protestant in America before the 1950s were given by their parents a copy of the King James Bible with dates in the margins. At the beginning of Genesis was 4004 BCE, the date for the creation of the world. The date was calculated by Archbishop James Ussher (1581–1656), head of the Anglican Church in Ireland and sometime professor at Trinity College, Dublin. He arrived at the date by adding up the years in the genealogies in Genesis and the reigns of the biblical kings, plus some other dates from what was known about the history of the Middle East. He went further to specify the date of creation as October 23, a Sunday.[4]

Ussher's date was similar to other calculations during the late Middle Ages, when Christians used the Bible for understanding nature. Most still thought the earth was the center of the universe, and Ussher probably heard when Rome in 1633 condemned Galileo for saying that the earth revolves around the sun. Ussher's 4004 BCE is close to the traditional calculation in Judaism, where the calendar starts with creation and where January 1 in 2000 CE was 5,760 years since the beginning. Such a recent date for creation is still prominent today in a calculation popular among some conservative Protestants, a Bible timeline.[5] It is seen also in Young Earth Creationism, which thinks the world is between 6,000 and 10,000 years old.

Ussher's date was used in the immensely influential the *Scofield Reference Bible*, published in 1909 and amplified in 1917, a volume that was to sell ten million copies and is still found today in Bible bookstores in a revised form. Cyrus I. Scofield, a Congregational minister and biblical scholar, compiled extensive and complicated notes to accompany a King James translation. He put 4004 BCE in the margin at Genesis 1 and then went on to add an interpretation that may be seen as a predecessor for what is today called Old Earth Creationism.

During the nineteenth century, Europeans and Americans were fascinated with natural history, prompted by exploration of the earth during the colonial era and by the development of sciences such as geology, paleontology, archaeology, and astronomy. Newspapers and magazines regularly carried stories about dinosaurs and other lost creatures, along with news from archaeological digs about early humans and humanlike mammals. Evidence increasingly mounted that the earth and its universe are very old and that life on earth evolved over a very long period of time.

By the beginning of the twentieth century, modernist (liberal) camps had developed in the Protestant denominations and within Roman Catholicism, and modernists had no trouble accepting both an old earth and evolution. Indeed, evolution had been accepted in some Christian circles before Darwin, for some had come to think of both human and natural history as developmental and changing.[6]

Conservative Protestants were troubled by evolution—many rejected it outright, but others, including some of the authors in *The Fundamentals*, offered limited acceptance. But on the issue of an old earth, by the beginning of the twentieth century many conservatives had found ways to accommodate an old earth with a literalist reading of Genesis. Scofield is an example.

Genesis 1:1 says in the King James translation, "God created the heaven and the earth." Using this translation, Scofield argued that Genesis 1:1 describes the first of two creations, an earlier creation that gave "scope to all the geologic ages." After this first creation, something went terribly wrong and the earth underwent "a cataclysmic change as the result of a divine judgment."[7] Genesis 1:2 tells us the result—"The earth was without form, and void; and darkness was upon the face of the deep." What went wrong? Scofield argued that the angels were part of this first creation, but Satan and other angels rebelled and brought God's harsh punishment upon the whole creation.[8] This view of a cataclysm in "a dateless past" allowed Scofield and his followers to accept geological evidence that the earth is very old and underwent upheavals in its past.

Then there was a second creation, allowing Scofield to introduce the Gap Theory. In this view, there were two creations with a gap between. Genesis 1:1 describes the first creation, and Genesis 1:3 begins the account of the second. It was the second creation that occurred in 4004 BCE, the creation that God accomplished in six days. By this imaginative interpretation, Scofield was able to accept scientific evidence of an old earth and still argue the literal accuracy of the story in Genesis.

FUNDAMENTALISTS, SCIENCE, AND DARWIN

The *Scofield Reference Bible* was a major building block in the growing fundamentalist edifice, and along with *The Fundamentals* and other publications of the time, it attempted to take science seriously. Indeed, in the nineteenth century there had been no question of science undermining Christianity but a question of how Christianity could use the new knowledge of the world coming from science. Most Protestants had welcomed the insights of such scientists as Isaac Newton, thinking that science could be used apologetically to support Christian claims.[9] A theme found at various points in Christian history has been that God is revealed in two books—in the book of scripture and in the book of nature. For many, the new scientific information about nature was giving support to the truths of the Bible, for the same God was seen in both books.[10]

Fundamentalism is based on a lust for certainty, and its view of science is related to this spirit. The Bible is understood to be a collection of factually accurate statements that may be understood by any Christian who reads it carefully. Likewise, nature is stable and predictable and displays clear facts about God's world that science is helping us to read. There is something populist about fundamentalism, for it is confident that average people can see the plain truth of the Bible and also see for themselves the magnificent harmonious system that God has designed into the earth and the universe.

Fundamentalism developed when the science associated with Isaac Newton was widely accepted, and it is still tied to this scientific view.[11] In Newtonian science, the universe operates like a well-ordered machine. The spectacular success with which scientists of that day predicted many astronomical phenomena seemed to demonstrate this, and there was growing confidence that all the created world could be seen as operating in a similar harmonious and predictable way. There were theological assumptions for many supporters of Newtonian science, for the ever-steady hand of God could be seen in both how the world was created and how it operates today. Fundamentalism fit easily into this worldview, for Newtonian science presented a model by which Christianity and science could exist side by side in harmony.

Charles Darwin and his 1859 *The Origin of Species* introduced changes in science that would accelerate in the twentieth century. Darwin wrote of natural selection, meaning living things in any group differ from one another and some are better adapted to their environment and more successful at reproducing. Through this natural selection, the earth has seen the evolution of an ever more complex array of living beings, including humans.[12]

Many Christians were very concerned that, unlike the Newtonian science they had grown up with, Darwin's science focused totally on the natural, leaving God out. Not only did natural selection not have God directing the process; it conflicted with the biblical idea that each living species was created directly by God. Some, recognizing that science was being separated from Christian ties, began to speak out against Darwin and to argue that the book of nature and the book of scripture must always agree. The seeds were sown for fundamentalism to add a crusade against Darwinian science to its crusade against biblical criticism that we saw in chapter 1.

A dramatic revolution in science occurred in the twentieth century, a revolution for which Darwin was a harbinger. From physics to genetics, from astronomy to anthropology and all of the other disciplines, science today pictures the world as dynamic and ever changing, built upon inner energy and motion rather than fixed building blocks, a world that in many ways is different from the way Newtonian science had described it. As Ian Barbour notes, "In place of immutable order, or change as rearrangement, nature is now understood to be evolutionary, dynamic, and emergent."[13] And most disturbing to some, this new science is no longer anthropocentric, for humans are seen not as God's special creation but as natural creatures that have evolved with all the rest. Here is a radically new model of nature, of science, and of humanity.

Against this new scientific view, some support what they call "creation science," an understanding of science and world related closely to the older Newtonian view and to Protestant fundamentalism. Some creationists are scientists with advanced degrees, but their science is at odds with most of today's science and usually they do not find places in major universities or research centers. Most work in fundamentalist colleges and in countercultural research centers established by fundamentalists around the country.

HENRY MORRIS AND THE INSTITUTE FOR CREATION RESEARCH

Publication of *The Genesis Flood* by John Whitcomb and Henry Morris in 1961 marked the beginning of the creationist movement as it is known today.[14] The book argues there is solid geological evidence that at one time a flood covered the whole earth, the flood described accurately in the Bible's story of Noah. "The waters which were above the firmament" (Gen 1:7 KJV) joined with the "fountains of the deep" (8:2 KJV) to flood the entire earth. Noah made an ark, a great ship calculated as having a deck of 95,700 square feet and capable of holding 35,000 individual vertebrate animals. Calm was maintained on the ark because God caused the animals to hibernate. Recognizing that most would not agree with the argument that the flood occurred about 3000 BCE and that the universe is fewer than 10,000 years old, the authors argue that God created an appearance of age as part of creation, to make it look old.[15] There also is a claim in the book that humans and dinosaurs lived at the same time and that there is evidence from an archaeological site in Texas.[16]

The Institute for Creation Research was established soon after the book was published, with Morris as director. The ICR became the chief voice for Young Earth Creationism, a position that came to be advocated by some school boards across the country and that ended up several times in the courts. Morris and the ICR have been dedicated fundamentalists—illustrated by an opening statement in *The Genesis Flood* that the Bible is the "infallible Word of God, verbally inspired" and by the ICR official tenets, which include an infallible Bible, a literal and historical six days of creation, and recognition of the harm done by the "humanistic evolution" that dominates America's science.[17]

The success of Morris and the ICR (and supporters of other types of creationism) has been possible because of changes in the religious landscape in America. After the Scopes trial of 1925, fundamentalists withdrew somewhat to themselves, disappointed with the trial and with the fact that public opinion in much of America seemed to go against them. At the time of the trial, fundamentalists had few institutions to support their cause, but that quickly changed.[18] A vigorous movement of Bible institutes and Bible colleges emerged as an alternative to the dozens of church-related colleges where both biblical criticism and Darwin were often taught and, of course, to the growing secular state-run colleges and universities.[19] Today tens of thousands of students are enrolled in dozens of Bible colleges where students are encouraged "to think biblically" and where the Bible is an integral part of all courses, including the sciences.[20] Further, fundamentalist books sell in the millions, often promoted in a network of Bible bookstores. Add to this the TV evangelists and their brand of conservative Christianity, plus thousands of private Christian elementary and high schools. Although not all fundamentalists are creationists, the movement is the base out of which creationism comes. And from this base have grown a number of organizations, study centers in Bible colleges, and now graduate programs and museums.

A YOUNG EARTH CREATIONIST READING OF GENESIS

For Henry Morris and his associates, the inerrant Bible does not need to be interpreted but simply read for its factual information, and when this is done it is obvious that creation took place in seven 24-hour days. Morris does not use Ussher's 4004 BCE but allows for a few more years for the generations in Genesis, coming up with about 10,000 years ago as the date for Adam and the creation.[21] Here are some of his details:

- Genesis 1:1 is the most important verse. Morris and others use the KJ and NIV, which unlike the NRSV, may be read as describing God creating in the first verse—"In the beginning God created the heavens and the earth" is the translation. Thus at the very outset, God brought into existence the entire space-mass-time universe ("heavens" in Genesis 1:1 means space, "earth" means mass, and "beginning" means time).[22] The verses that follow are an elaboration and continuation of this key verse.

- The story tells us that God created plants and trees on day three but the sun was not put in the sky until day four. How can vegetation survive without sunlight? Morris says that God created light plus the day and night cycle on day one, as part of heaven. There was a special light (now unknown to us) that operated until the sun was created on day four.[23]

- All was created by God's command, and all living kinds that exist today came into being during that short week. Genesis 1 uses *bara* (kind) ten times to describe types of plants and animals. Although there is the possibility of some variation and even small changes in a kind (for example, skin color in humans, types of dogs), a kind was fixed by "special creation" at the beginning and one kind does not evolve out of another.[24] The emphasis on kinds is the foundation for a vehement rejection of Darwinian evolution and for an insistence that humans did not evolve from other mammals.

- There was no death in the human or animal world of the original Paradise until Adam and Eve sinned by eating the forbidden fruit. Animals and humans were vegetarians in the garden, so animal death was not necessary to produce food. This view of death is reinforced when Paul says in Romans 5:12 that death entered the world because of sin.[25]

- Where did the sons of Adam and Eve get their wives? This is an old problem, and for this Morris's associate Duane Gish interprets. Moses tells us in Genesis 5:4 that Adam had sons and daughters, so the sons took their sisters as wives. This necessary expediency was possible because the first humans had no genetic defects and their children would have been normal.[26]

THE CREATION MUSEUM

A major museum opened in 2007 to give support to Young Earth Creationism—the Creation Museum, located outside Cincinnati in northern Kentucky. Constructed at a cost of $27 million, the museum is intended to be an alternative to the natural history museums found in major cities, all of which support Darwinian evolution. The Creation Museum claims to show that Genesis accurately describes how the world began, advancing its view by picturing major stories from Genesis through animated scenes that remind some of a Disney theme park. Visitors may walk through an exhibit of Noah's ark, seeing Noah and his supporters raising the beams while nearby animal pairs are being gathered on two floors. Another exhibit shows early human children playing happily among dinosaurs, for both humans and dinosaurs were created on the sixth day and lived peacefully for generations. The claim throughout is that every word of Genesis is literally true, that creation occurred 6,000 years ago, and that there is solid scientific evidence to support what is presented.

Among the exhibits is "Culture in Crisis," where visitors are invited to look into today's average home to see young people indulge in drugs, pornography, and abortion, while nearby a church has been damaged by a "millions of years" wrecking ball. The museum argues that much of the misery faced by people today is the result of the replacement of the truth of God's word in Genesis by the evolutionary views advanced by today's scientists and accepted by many churches.

The Creation Museum is sponsored by Answers in Genesis, a fundamentalist organization with views similar to those of the Institute for Creation Research. A number of scientists have raised concerns, for they anticipate that young people will be influenced by the museum's graphic and entertaining exhibits and thus come to science classes in high schools and colleges with views both hostile and incorrect. Over 800 scientists from colleges and universities in the states near the museum—Ohio, Indiana, Kentucky—have issued a statement warning of the "scientifically inaccurate materials" in the exhibits.[27]

AN OLD EARTH CREATIONIST READING OF GENESIS

Often creationism is identified with Henry Morris, the Institute for Creation Research, and their Young Earth Creationism. There is also a position called Old Earth Creationism, and its supporters disagree with Morris and think a day in Genesis was not like our 24 hours. They argue that a day in the Bible *may* mean 24 hours, but in some places (as in Genesis 1) it means a longer period of time. This "day-age" view was the most popular among conservative Protestants from the nineteenth century up to the 1960s and has been the view of a wide variety of Christians—from Augustine to William Jennings Bryan to Billy Graham.

Prominent among Old Earth Creationists is Hugh Ross and his research organization, Reasons to Believe. Ross is a fundamentalist, like his Young Earth counterparts, and he thinks the Bible is completely without error, historically or scientifically. He rejects natural biological evolution and is adamantly opposed to Darwinism, yet he finds reasons to think Genesis is compatible with a very old universe. Here are a few of his points:

- Ross accepts the view of most scientists that a Big Bang started the universe almost 14 billion years ago and that the earth is about 4.5 billion years old. Morris and his associates reject the Big Bang.

- Unlike Morris, Ross thinks Noah's flood covered only the Near East. He thus meets the objections of scientists that the earth has never had enough water for a universal flood.
- Adam and Eve lived 30,000 to 50,000 years ago, and their dates are compatible with the Genesis record if it is recognized that the biblical genealogies cover only the most important people, leaving out a number of generations. Disagreeing with Morris, Ross thinks death did not start with Adam and Eve but was part of the animal world from the beginning.
- Ross argues that the sun was created as part of the heavens of Genesis 1:1 and so was available to give energy to the plants on day three, before the sun became visible through the cloud cover on day four.[28]

In spite of its obvious disagreements with the new Creation Museum, the Reasons to Believe organization has avoided any criticism of the exhibits, arguing instead that the focus should be on what the several creationist positions have in common.

THE DIVIDING LINE BETWEEN CREATIONISTS AND OTHER CHRISTIANS

We have discussed the Gap Theory, Young Earth Creationism, and Old Earth Creationism. Although there is not a single creationist view, behind their disagreements creationists do share two things: (1) a belief that Genesis is giving accurate factual details about the creation, a belief that grows out of a fundamentalist way of reading the Bible, and (2) a conviction that the views of Charles Darwin and his followers must be vigorously opposed because they contradict the inerrant facts about creation set forth in Genesis.

Advocates of these creationist views have a large number of Americans on their side. It is helpful again to look at the results of a Gallup poll, which asked a question that may be identified with Young Earth Creationism. The statement was "God created human beings pretty much in their present form at one time within the last 10,000 years or so," and 46 percent of American respondents agreed.[29] It is obvious that many millions of Americans are creationists, whether or not they identify with the term.

It is also true that millions disagree with creationists. The same Gallup poll found that 36 percent of Americans agreed with a very different statement, "Human beings have developed over millions of years from less advanced forms of life, but God guided this process." This second statement is in line with the positions of mainline Protestant churches and of the Roman Catholic Church, institutions that have considerable respect and influence. In the minds of millions of people in the pews of these churches, there is no hostility between Christianity and modern science and the hatchet was buried decades ago. This irenic picture in much of Christianity is illustrated in the dozens of dialogue groups around the country in which theologians and church leaders participate alongside practicing scientists in attempts to promote mutual respect and understanding.[30]

Creationists often say the debate is between biblical Christianity and modern Darwinian science. *Their claim here is misleading, for the debate is better understood as a debate between two different kinds of Christianity and two very different approaches to understanding Genesis.* We now turn to the views of those Christians who reject the creationist approach.

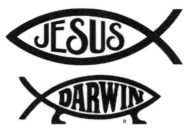

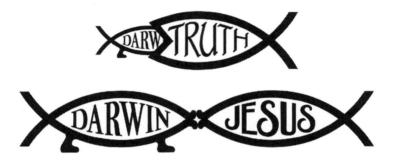

JESUS FISH, DARWIN FISH

Early Christians used a fish to symbolize Jesus Christ, and often today's evangelicals put "Jesus" in an outline of a fish. Some scientists, responding to creationists, put feet on a Darwin fish to affirm evolution. Creationists have responded by picturing Jesus as Truth consuming Darwin. Biologist Kenneth Miller, seeing no conflict between his Roman Catholic Christianity and his science, suggests kissing fish. (Graphics prepared by Catherine Jennings. Darwin Fish is a registered trademark of Evolution Design, Inc. Karnes City, Texas and is used with the owner's permission.)

THE POSITION
OF MAINLINE CHURCHES

At a 1981 trial in Little Rock, Arkansas, a trial to decide whether creationism should be taught in Arkansas public schools, a remarkable group lined up *against* creationism. It included the bishops in Arkansas for the United Methodist Church, the Episcopal Church, the Roman Catholic Church, and the African Methodist Episcopal Church, plus the principal official of the largest Presbyterian denomination in Arkansas and the leaders of three Jewish organizations. Methodist bishop Kenneth W. Hicks was articulate on the stand in saying that a law passed by the Arkansas legislature would inject a creationist reading of Genesis into the public schools and thereby violate the rights of Methodists and others who do not agree with a fundamentalist reading of the Bible.[31]

Mainline Protestant churches in America, along with the Roman Catholic Church, have taken stands against creationism. For some of these churches, the anti-creationist position may be seen in official statements, for others more indirectly as they consider how to interpret the Bible. We note two churches here.

The Presbyterian Church (USA) may serve as an example from the mainline Protestant churches. This was the Protestant body that a century ago in its northern branch adopted the Five Points, thereby advocating biblical inerrancy, and this was the church most torn by the fundamentalist controversy. Recognizing this heritage, a Presbyterian study in 1969 officially concluded

> that the true relation between the evolutionary theory and the Bible is that of noncontradiction and that the position stated by the General Assemblies of 1886, 1888,

1889 and 1924—which had interpreted Scripture as being opposed to the theory of evolution—was in error and
no longer represents the mind of our Church.[32]

Further, in a 1982 statement concerning the interpretation
of Genesis, the church affirms

the imposition of a fundamentalist viewpoint about the
interpretation of Biblical literature—where every word
is taken with uniform literalness and becomes an absolute authority on all matters, whether moral, religious,
political, historical or scientific—is in conflict with the
perspective on Biblical interpretation characteristically
maintained by Biblical scholars and theological schools
in the mainstream of Protestantism, Catholicism, and
Judaism. Such scholars find that the scientific theory of
evolution does not conflict with their interpretation of
the origins of life found in Biblical literature.[33]

This statement also put Presbyterians on record as opposing
attempts by the Institute for Creation Research to encourage
state legislatures to introduce the teaching of creation science
in the public schools.

The Roman Catholic Church has not been burdened with
fundamentalism as Protestant churches have. It is the Protestant principle of *sola scriptura* (the Bible alone) that has almost
guaranteed that Protestants would disagree about how to understand what they claim to be the one source for their religion.
Catholic tradition has augmented the Bible with the traditional
teachings of the church, and sometimes it is "papal fundamentalism" that troubles some Catholics. On the issue of whether
Christians may accept Darwinian evolution, the statements of

popes and other leaders may be as important to Catholics as the book of Genesis.

The Catholic Church was early suspicious of evolution and Darwin's ideas because of a concern that evolution implied materialism to the exclusion of any spiritual dimension. The 1950 encyclical *Humani Generis* was a watershed, for it gave tentative approval to evolutionary ideas. Concerning the possibility of human evolution, Pope Pius XII wrote, "Evolution is an open question, as long as it confines its speculation to the development, from other living matter already in existence, of the human body." Then, adding something peculiarly Catholic, he said that "souls are immediately created by God" and inserted into human bodies. It should be recalled from chapter 1 that this is the pope who in 1943 accepted modern methods of biblical scholarship, thus liberating Catholics from a literalist reading of the Genesis creation stories.

Pope John Paul II pushed his church further into an acceptance of evolution, and his statements are often cited by scientists and theologians. In a 1996 speech to the Pontifical Academy of Sciences, the pope noted that Pius XII had recognized evolution as a "serious hypothesis" and added that in the years since *Humani Generis* it has become "more than a hypothesis" and has become a theory widely accepted by researchers. Continuing his church's concern that some understand evolution as reducing life to a purely materialistic process, John Paul noted that humans have a special place, created in the image of God and with spiritual souls "immediately created by God." He said humans have a "physical continuity" with the rest of nature but also an "ontological discontinuity."[34]

Benedict XVI became pope in 2005, and many are awaiting his views about evolution, although some are on record from the years when he was Cardinal Ratzinger. In 2004 an important study called *Communion and Stewardship* was published with the cardinal's approval. It contains a yes-but approach to Darwin's idea of chance variation, saying that "true contingency in the created order is not incompatible with a purposeful divine providence." God created the world with the chance variations that scientists describe, and "divine causality can be active in a process that is *both* contingent and guided," according to the man who became pope.[35]

JOHN HAUGHT
AND A GOD WHO "LETS BE"

Many Christian scholars today deal with the issues raised by today's science, often at considerable length. Our example is John Haught, a professor of theology at Georgetown University and a scholar whose views are widely read. Haught is Roman Catholic, but he would also be at home in many Protestant circles. He was a key witness against creationism and Intelligent Design at the 2005 *Kitzmiller* court case, which declared Intelligent Design unconstitutional.

For Haught, Darwin's "dangerous ideas" are not a threat but a gift that challenges Christians to develop new understandings of God and how God creates.[36] He thinks the traditional "benign, ordering deity" of Western theology is no longer appropriate in the light of today's evolutionary understandings. To use language from our last chapter, Haught moves beyond classical theism and shares many of the ideas we have identified with panentheism.

Central to Haught's analysis is the relationship between God's *power* and God's *love*.

Traditionally, Western religions have focused on the omnipotence of God, imagining an all-powerful God who in creation controls and directs the process. Haught thinks the direct exercise of great power cannot be harmonized with God's love, for true love refrains from coercive manipulation, it encourages independence, it "lets be." Darwin and his followers describe a world that evolves without the intervention of God, a world molded by random variation, by natural selection, by experimentation. Haught thinks Christians must accept this understanding of the world by recognizing that God withholds his power so the universe may evolve and develop on its own.[37]

Haught focuses on St. Paul's statement in Philippians 2:7 that God "emptied himself" in coming to earth as the man Jesus. Reflecting the Greek word, this *kenotic* theology of an emptying God is a springboard for ideas about God, ideas that are developed in detail in the panentheistic theology that we have noted. Haught says that in creation, motivated by love, God encourages the world to develop independently. God retreats, even humbles himself, so that the world may be filled with novelty and experimentation and change and ever-exciting newness. The universe is not planned or controlled by this God.[38]

How about humans? Humanity evolved from earlier mammals, and we cannot back away from this reality. Both Pope Pius XII and Pope John Paul II recognized this, but both insisted that God infuses souls into human bodies, making humans different. Haught does not like this formulation and says that Darwin compels us to reexamine the idea of soul. If humans have souls, then all living beings also have something analogous to a soul. The Latin word for soul is *anima*, which is basically an animating principle, so we may recognize that all living things are "ensouled."[39]

What does Haught say about Genesis? He does not present a detailed commentary, but there are many passing references to Genesis in his writings. Noting that Daniel Dennett writes that "Darwin's idea has banished the Book of Genesis to the limbo of quaint mythology," Haught disagrees sharply.[40]

> Genesis . . . seeks to awaken in us a sense of gratitude for
> the sheer glory and extravagance of creation. It tells us,
> in two distinct accounts, that the universe is grounded in
> love and promise. It provides us with a reason to hope. It
> assures us, moreover, that our world is essentially good
> and that nature is not to be confused with God.[41]

Unfortunately, Haught says, some still attempt to find scientific accuracy in Genesis and, by doing this, diminish the religious power of the texts. The symbols and metaphors of Genesis still live and may lead us deeper into the world of the spirit than is possible with any literal reading.

Haught and other Christians supporting Darwin argue against two extremes. They reject creation science and creationist readings of Genesis. But they also do not like the naturalistic evolution that paints a materialistic picture with no place for religion, a view found among not a few scientists and reflected in Carl Sagan's famous statement that "the cosmos is all that is or ever was or ever will be."[42] For Haught the creation may never be understood properly apart from the grace of the God who makes it all possible.

JEWISH VIEWS

Opposition to creationism is found in all branches of American Judaism. The Reform branch of Judaism has issued statements opposing creationist views and praising legal decisions keeping these out of the schools.[43] The Rabbinical Council of America in a statement on creationism says that "evolutionary theory, properly understood, is not incompatible with . . . the first 2 chapters of Genesis." The Council, which represents Orthodox rabbis, quotes Maimonides in saying that "what the

Torah writes about the Account of Creation is not all to be taken literally."[44] From left to right and all areas in between, there is widespread rejection of creationism.[45]

Most important, the very approach of creationism goes against the Jewish ways of reading the Bible that were noted in Chapter 1. There is a long tradition of reading Genesis that does not take a literalist approach and that emphasizes an Oral Torah in which new meanings and insights are sought. Further, much of Judaism considers the Torah to be self-sufficient and not in need of outside insights, so it would clearly reject the idea that a creation science can validate what is in the creation stories.[46]

Also, Jews have been politically active in America, defending the rights of Jews as a minority. They remember the time when in many parts of the country public schools were operated like Protestant parochial schools and judge correctly that creationists would reintroduce conservative Protestant themes. Jews have been strong defenders of the First Amendment and have long thought that non-Christians will be treated fairly only when the government is staunchly neutral in affairs of religion.

ENTER INTELLIGENT DESIGN

Intelligent Design is a movement that entered the public debate in the early nineties.[47] The Discovery Institute, a major supporter, notes its characteristics:

> The scientific theory of Intelligent Design holds that certain features of the universe and of living things are best explained by an intelligent cause, not an undirected process such as natural selection. The intelligent cause does not have to be a divine being.

ID accepts evolution, if this simply means change over time and common ancestry. Yet in disagreement with much of today's science, ID sees intervention by an intelligent cause at key points in the evolutionary process. It strongly objects to neo-Darwinian views that change occurs by natural selection in a purposeless process that has no discernable direction or goal.[48]

Intelligent Design has been widely identified with creationism. It has been called "Intelligent Design creationism," "born-again creationism,"[49] and "creationism lite."[50] Its supporters have been called "neo-creos."[51] In the 2005 *Kitzmiller* opinion, in a case dealing with whether ID could be introduced into the public schools, Judge John E. Jones concluded that Intelligent Design is a form of creationism.

Supporters insist that ID is *not* creationism. They say they are not interested in defending Genesis, and even though many supporters are Christians, ID itself is agnostic regarding the question of God as the designer. The intellectual roots of the movement are varied, with influences coming from such giants as Plato and Aristotle as well as from Christian and Jewish thinkers. And, most of all, supporters state that ID must be recognized as a scientific theory that stands totally apart from religious commitments.[52]

Many ID supporters consider the claims of creationism to be outlandish. An example is Michael Behe, a biologist and one of the most-quoted ID supporters, a scholar who, like John Haught, testified at the 2005 *Kitzmiller* court case. A Roman Catholic and no fundamentalist, Behe makes an occasional reference to what a pope says about evolution but no reference to Genesis. His focus is on Darwinian theory, which he partly accepts but on balance finds inadequate. Darwin's theory of natural selection may explain many things, but it cannot explain molecular life. As a scientist, Behe says, he must recognize the intervention of an outside intelligence at key points in the evolutionary process.[53] While the outside intelligence for him is the Christian God, he recognizes it might be understood in different ways, including perhaps a visit by intelligent beings from elsewhere in the universe.

Defenders of Intelligent Design insist it is not creationism; some critics say it is. Which position is correct? To answer this question, it is helpful to consider two themes of creationism considered earlier—a focus on Genesis and a rejection of Darwin.

First, if creationism is based on a reading of Genesis, then Intelligent Design is not creationism. A perusal of the literature by ID advocates shows almost no interest in Genesis. After coming this far in our study, with numerous lively debates about interpreting Genesis, with ID there are very few such debates.[54] Further, Intelligent Design has a different approach to Darwinian science than does creationism. Like creationism, ID finds serious problems with natural selection and vigorously challenges some aspects of prevailing scientific orthodoxy. But unlike creationism, ID does accept evolution.

While agreeing with Judge Jones that Intelligent Design is a religious more than a scientific theory and so has no place in the public schools, we should also support the claim of its supporters that ID is different from creationism.[55]

CONCLUSION

In this chapter we have seen how creationism is related to Newtonian science, a science that focuses on the order and harmony of a machinelike universe, a science that works from an underlying model of a *fixed and stable universe*. In contrast to this is a model that understands all that exists as *dynamic and evolving*, a way of thinking that is at the heart of prevailing science today and that also lies back of biblical criticism and its understanding that the Bible came out of the flow of Near

Eastern history. *Biblical criticism and Darwinism share a view that all existence is dynamic and evolving, while creationism and Newtonian science think in terms of the fixed and stable.* This contrast lies back of the debates about Genesis.

Creationists do recognize some movement and change in life, but back of it all is a God who is changeless, a God who created a world that at its deepest level reflects the nature of its creator in being stable. For creationists there also are eternal and unchanging truths and a Bible that comes from God and conveys many of these truths, including information about how the world began. Creationists stand firm in their rocklike conviction that at the core of life are things, which like God do not change with time, things such as the "kinds" of creatures described in Genesis 1. And they find an ally in what they consider to be the only true science, a creation science in the Newtonian mold.

The view that we have advocated is very different. Yes, there are continuing insights and wisdom from the Bible, and these must be studied and championed. At the same time, we know that existence is always changing and that living things have evolved from other living things and continue to evolve. We are forever on a pilgrimage toward an open future and cannot escape the reality that religious understandings of both God and world change over time and are influenced by the events and outlooks of each new age. In this light, many Jews and Christians today welcome the ideas of Charles Darwin and have come to read the creation stories in ways that are compatible with evolution. This entails an understanding of both the world and God in terms of *dynamic and evolving* interrelationships.

THE CREATION STORIES IN THE PUBLIC ARENA

"WE THE PEOPLE . . ." is inscribed across the front of the National Constitution Center in Philadelphia, and these opening words of the Preamble to the Constitution of the United States resonate in the programs and exhibits to be found inside. "In the beginning . . ." serves as a preamble to the Hebrew Bible, and these words also are found in exhibits inside the Constitution Center. "We the people" through our courts at times are called upon to adjudicate how the "in the beginning" stories are to be handled in the public arena.

Religion in America often is not confined to individuals or religious communities, and continues to be an important part of the social discourse. The creation stories lie at an intersection where the views of religiously committed people often touch the rough-and-tumble life of the larger society. At this intersection a number of interpretations may be heard, some more loudly than others but all proclaiming their view of the stories to be of great importance. No wonder, then, that the creation stories are at the heart of so much disagreement about religion.

To conclude, and to illustrate how the stories come to play in the public arena, let us comment on some themes that have run through our study.

First, look at the word "God." It seems as American as apple pie. It is expected from preachers, priests, and rabbis; it is heard from politicians; it is stamped on American coins and collective identity; and from opinion polls, consistently 90 percent or more of Americans confess a belief in God. "One nation under God" is part of a pledge to the flag that most grew up with, and it goes along with a common view that all people worship the same God. But what does "God" mean? Most Americans seem to think God is self-evident, and if their silence is pushed, they are likely to say something implying a classical theism with its transcendent Father God.

Such a religio-political confession violates the beliefs of millions of Americans. Even from within Judaism and Christianity, we have seen that some do not accept the traditional idea of God and even think it does harm. Humans speak metaphorically and anthropologically of God, and words about God never accurately describe the reality. God-language is forever inadequate, history is littered with dead ideas about God, and new understandings are periodically introduced. In our study we have seen the increasingly influential view known as panentheism and its attempts to talk of God and universe in one breath, not two. Add long-ignored female characteristics to God, along with the proposal that the creation stories should be amended with descriptions of the creator as Mother. Further, there is the intriguing suggestion that God humbly steps back and allows the universe to unfold in dynamic evolutionary serendipity, rather than lording over it all in power. Much is going on in Judaism and Christianity in attempts to understand what is in this simple word "God."

It must also be recognized that America is becoming increasingly pluralistic and that today there is a significant religious presence beyond the original American faiths. Protestant-Catholic-Jew was the description a generation ago; now it is more accurately Protestant-Catholic-Jew-Muslim-Buddhist-Hindu-Taoist-Sikh-Zoroastrian-American Indian, and a host of others.[1] Most of these new religions have views of the divine very different from the traditional God of the West. For Hinduism and American Indian religions there are various deities, and for many Buddhists there are no gods in any traditional sense. Even for Muslims, who share the monotheism of the West, ideas about God often are very different from those of many Jews and Christians. And there are increasing numbers of agnostics and atheists whose religious honesty must be respected and encouraged.

Americans must accept religious pluralism and recognize that the God of "in the beginning when God" as well as of "one nation under God" may mean radically different things for different people or may be part of a monotheism that increasing numbers do not accept.

Alternate creation stories will increasingly be told, and these will challenge the near-monopoly the Genesis stories have held. Out of the new religious pluralism in America come other creation stories very different from the two in Genesis, and these will increasingly be heard. Here are two examples.

Hinduism in its stories talks of a continuous and unending cyclical process by which all existence winds up and runs down and winds up and runs down in an endless flow. There are stories in Hinduism that tell how the gods created the universe, but these stories tell only of our penultimate world. Ultimately for much of Hinduism there is no beginning or ending, and there are other universes in an infinite and incomprehensible reality. The "in the beginning" of the Bible, if it means anything for a Hindu, cannot mean a onetime event but only the start of one age among many.

Another alternative to Genesis is found in the creation stories of the American Indian people, stories that have been here all along but are now gaining wider audiences and respect. Some of these stories tell of life coming from within the earth, graphically illustrated by the kivas of the Pueblo people of the American Southwest. A kiva is a womblike structure, sometimes built partially into the earth. In the kiva is a small hole called a sipapu, which is symbolically the passage to the next womb down, which is for some connected to still another womb. Symbolically, all life (humans and their nonhuman relatives) comes from deep within Mother Earth, which is the source of all that lives. Kiva ceremonies and accompanying dances are being revived today in the Southwest with considerable vigor. Most Indian tribes do not have kiva-based religions, but all focus on the sacredness of the earth and so have a focus that is very different from traditional understandings of the Genesis stories.

Next, how is the Bible to be understood? The Bible has played an important role in American history, going back to the early Puritans and extending through the speeches of Abraham Lincoln and later presidents. At one time readings from the Bible were common in the public schools and some would put the Bible back in the schools. Because for some conservative Christians the Bible is God's Word without error, a surprising number of Americans still think that Genesis and not Darwin should be our guide for how human life began. Protestantism with its dual emphasis on "the Bible alone" and "the priesthood of all believers" has been democratic in spirit and has led many

Americans to think it is relatively easy for anyone to read and understand the Bible.

Harold Bloom argues that "the Bible is the most difficult of all difficult books" and says that it is almost impossible to read without help from scholarly experts.[2] Such a claim is a little too elitist, for there have always been nonscholars who have through their own efforts been able to penetrate the complexities of the Bible and develop a depth of understanding. But Bloom's claim does have considerable validity, for this is a difficult book that is best read with the help of those who spend their lives studying its pages. Biblical scholars usually come out of faith communities, and scholars are indispensable when others in that community attempt to understand the Bible. Judaism has always known this, for well-educated rabbis have for centuries served as scholarly guides to their people in understanding the Hebrew scriptures and the complex history of interpretation. Catholics and Protestants would be well served by doing more to follow this Jewish example.

Sadly, most Americans are unaware of biblical criticism and the advances in understanding the Bible in the last century and beyond. Fundamentalist claims have been loudly advanced, and for many that is all that is known. Langdon Gilkey, the late theologian from the University of Chicago, provides an anecdote to illustrate. He was to testify at the creationist trial in Little Rock when he was approached by a reporter from *Time* magazine who thought that Gilkey, a Christian, was obviously supporting the creationist cause. Gilkey told the man that since he was so ignorant about biblical scholarship, he should not be covering the trial! We must with Gilkey bemoan the fact that even educated people in America are unaware of what is going on in biblical scholarship. And, Gilkey went on, Christian clergy sadly have done little to introduce to their people scholarly methods of Bible study.[3]

The creation stories are an important part of America's public and religious heritage, and the work of Jewish and Christian biblical scholars is invaluable. Americans would be well served by a better understanding of the kind of biblical scholarship we have considered.

With the creation stories, religion meets politics, science, culture, commerce, education, and a host of things that go beyond the individual. A number of examples could be cited where the stories end up, for good or for harm, in a public area. Such was the decision of America's astronauts on the first moon voyage, *Apollo 8*, to read the creation stories from space. On Christmas Eve, 1968, the three astronauts took turns reading the first ten verses of Genesis for a vast global television audience, thus tying the biblical stories with America's scientific and political agenda.[4]

Another example is found in the natural history museums that have become increasingly popular, museums that usually have programs on how stars and planets are born, plus displays documenting the evolution of life on earth. The museum exhibits are silent about creation stories from the Bible or other religious traditions, but stories of creation are in the museums nonetheless in the minds of many who visit. The exhibits almost cry out for a dialogue to fill the void. This dialogue does take place in the few programs sponsored by the museums and more often in ongoing discussions about science and religion within America's religious institutions.[5]

With the Genesis stories, entanglements with a host of areas that extend beyond the individual cannot be avoided, as has been seen clearly in our study. The recognition that religion has truly large implications is a refreshing counterbalance to much of the narcissism in American religion. Often the focus is on personal faith and individual salvation, on a purpose driven life in which one finds meaning in the midst of an otherwise largely meaningless existence. The creation stories insist that humans take the big view they proclaim that individuals may find meaning only in relation to the whole. They envision a cosmos, something too often missing in America's religions.

Finally, a few concluding comments. Our study is appropriately called *Storms over Genesis*. Every page has dealt with disagreements, as the creation stories have been the focus of debates both within religious communities and in the larger public arena. The stories themselves have stood up well in the debates. Jews and Christians who have struggled with interpreting the stories have often developed valuable insights and would say the process should continue.

The storms we have dealt with have been a product of the twentieth century, a century that was marked by some of the worst and some of the best in the human experience. The century saw the greatest destruction in all recorded history—humans killing other humans in fantastic numbers through wars and holocausts, a killing matched by massive human destruction of the natural environment. The century also produced much that was positive—the rising place for people of color and for females and for the lower classes, plus the explosion of knowledge and efforts to improve the human situation. *In both the worst and the best of this past century, the focus was on the human.*

Now we are in the twenty-first century. As the creation stories continue to be discussed and debated, no doubt the issues will be different. *In this century the focus will shift partly away from the human and toward "the heavens and the earth."* Already there has been expanded knowledge of the outer reaches of our universe, and in this new century infant space sciences will mature and produce fantastic new ways of understanding our universe and universes beyond. Meanwhile, the human relationship with the earth will also change, both because the earth will demand it and because humans will develop new ways of seeing their place in their world. In both the "heavens" and the "earth" parts of this new focus, the creation stories will have a key role, as Jews and Christians struggle with their understandings of their God and the beneficent world that is this God's gift.

NOTES ON THE NRSV

Since the New Revised Standard Version is used in this study, two areas where the NRSV departs from older translations should be noted. Both are important in the debates.

THE TRANSLATION OF GENESIS 1:1

The first departure is the translation of the first verse. The key word "when" shows that the NRSV interprets the first two verses to be describing conditions before creation began, thereby setting the stage for creation to begin with "God said" in verse 3.

> [1]In the beginning *when* God created the heavens and the earth, [2]the earth was a formless void. . . . (italics added here and in other quotes from Genesis, for emphasis)

By comparison to the NRSV, note other popular translations:

> [1]In the beginning God created the heaven and the earth.
> [2]And the earth was without form, and void. . . . (KJ, 1611)

¹In the beginning God created the heavens and the earth.
²The earth was without form and void. . . . (RSV, 1952)

¹In the beginning God created the heavens and the earth.
²Now the earth was formless and empty. . . . (NIV, 1978)

Disagreement with the NRSV comes mostly from conservative Protestant circles, for an official Roman Catholic translation and a popular Jewish translation agree with the NRSV and use "when."

¹In the beginning, *when* God created the heavens and the earth, the earth was a formless wasteland. . . . (NAB, 1970, Roman Catholic)

¹*When* God began to create heaven and earth—²the earth being unformed and void. . . . (TANAKH, 1985, Jewish)

The key issue in the translation is whether God is creating in the first verse. Seeing a proclamation ("God created") and a sentence ending with a period in some translations, some say that God is creating in verse 1. The NRSV interprets the first two verses to be describing conditions before God created. This difference in translation is important for the discussions in the chapter on creationism.

INCLUSIVE LANGUAGE

The use of inclusive language is a second major departure. The NRSV was the first major translation to recognize that the English language is biased toward males and that this bias seeps into many Bible translations. The translators thus sought to use inclusive language when the original text clearly implies both males and females. Note what inclusive language does in Genesis 1:26, compared to familiar earlier translations.

> Then God said, "Let us make *humankind* in our image." (NRSV)

> Then God said, "Let us make *man* in our image." (KJ, RSV, NAB, NIV)

The New Revised Standard Version was an ecumenical project of thirty biblical scholars who represented several Protestant denominations, Orthodox churches, the Roman Catholic Church, and Judaism. The instructions from the sponsoring National Council of Churches included a directive to change or soften wherever possible the male bias found in the English of the popular Revised Standard Version of 1952. Obviously the influence of feminists in many churches was back of these instructions.

The NRSV quickly gained popularity and may today be found in the Sunday services of mainline Protestant churches all over the country, in some Roman Catholic circles, and in Bible study in colleges and universities as well as in churches. It is the translation of choice in the majority of scholarly works in which the Bible is cited.

Meanwhile, the conservative evangelical Protestant movement was growing. Among evangelicals there was some dissatisfaction with the RSV, which became an outright rejection of the NRSV when it appeared. This rejection is based in part on the NRSV's treatment of the Genesis creation stories—specifically the two departures we have noted, inclusive language and the translation of Genesis 1:1. Evangelicals prefer the New

International Version, a translation produced in 1978 by a team of evangelical scholars.[1] The NIV is today the best-selling Bible in the English language.

A battle is now raging *within* evangelical ranks on the question of inclusive language. There are vocal evangelical feminists, and a strong minority wants an inclusive-language Bible, which the NIV is not. Such a translation appeared in 2005 as Today's New International Version, which has for Genesis 1:26: "Then God said, 'Let us make *human beings* in our image.' Some evangelicals quickly condemned the TNIV as a dangerous sellout to feminists, and battle lines within evangelical ranks were set. Evangelical publications addressed the issue, many opposing but some seeking a balanced discussion.[2] The largest Protestant body in America, the 16-million-member Southern Baptist Convention, which supports the NIV, at its 2002 convention condemned the soon-to-be-published TNIV and advised its members to avoid it.[3] Among mainline Protestants, there is little debate about inclusive language, but among evangelicals the disagreement is heated.

Meanwhile, Roman Catholics have become involved. Catholic bishops, in an ecumenical spirit, have at times approved for use by Catholics translations sponsored primarily by Protestants. In 1991 the Roman Catholic bishops in the United States officially approved the NRSV and its inclusive language for use in Catholic services. This action was forwarded to Rome for final approval, but in 1994 the Congregation for the Doctrine of the Faith said no to the NRSV. A church official said the rejection was because of inclusive language. The head of the congregation at that time was Cardinal Joseph Ratzinger, the man who is now Pope Benedict XVI.[4]

In spite of this rejection, there has been support for the NRSV in some Catholic circles. The Catholic Biblical Association of America expressed support for the bishops' approval of the NRSV and dismay at Rome's veto.[5] And the Dominican monks at St. John's Monastery in Minnesota are moving ahead on their ambitious project of producing the first Bible to be written and illuminated entirely by hand in 500 years. For the *St. John's Bible* the monks chose an English translation, the NRSV.[6]

COURT CASES INVOLVING GENESIS

TENNESSEE V. JOHN THOMAS SCOPES, A 1925 UNITED STATES STATE COURT OPINION

The 1925 Butler Act in Tennessee prohibited public school teachers from teaching "any theory that denies the story of the Divine Creation of man as taught in the Bible." To challenge the law, the American Civil Liberties Union found a volunteer in John Scopes, a teacher who was charged with breaking the law after he admitted discussing Darwin's ideas in class. In the courtroom were two famous Americans—biblical fundamentalist and sometime Democratic presidential candidate William Jennings Bryan supporting the law, and prominent trial lawyer and agnostic Clarence Darrow defending Scopes. By all accounts the Scopes "monkey trial" and surrounding events were like a carnival.

Dayton, Tennessee, and its trial received worldwide press coverage, most of which was negative toward the fundamentalist position. Scopes was convicted, as expected, and fined

$100. The ACLU had hoped to appeal to the United States Supreme Court, but that was not possible because the Tennessee Supreme Court threw the conviction out on a technicality and there was no retrial. The Tennessee legislature repealed the law in 1967.

Beginning in 1960, Americans have come to know the trial primarily through a popular movie, *Inherit the Wind*. In several aspects the movie is an inaccurate depiction, especially in the portrayal of Bryan. Bryan did take the stand as an expert in the Bible, but the movie is incorrect in having Bryan agree with Bishop Ussher that the creation occurred in 4004 BCE. On the stand Bryan actually said the six days of Genesis could be six years or six million years or 600 million years.

A helpful analysis of the trial is by Edward J. Larson, *Summer of the Gods: The Scopes Trial and America's Continuing Debate over Science and Religion* (New York: Basic, 1977).

EPPERSON V. ARKANSAS, A 1968 UNITED STATES SUPREME COURT OPINION

This case involved a law in Arkansas similar to that in Tennessee under which Scopes was tried. In 1928 Arkansas adopted a law making it unlawful for any teacher in a state-supported school or university to teach "that mankind ascended or descended from a lower order of animals." The challenge was brought in the name of Susan Epperson, a high school biology teacher who wished to use a textbook that included Darwinian theory. All nine justices ruled against the Arkansas law.

Justice Abe Fortas delivered the opinion of the court, arguing that the law was promoting a religious viewpoint and thus was a violation of the Establishment Clause of the First Amendment. The justice wrote, "It is clear that fundamentalist sectarian conviction was and is the law's reason for existence," and further noted that evolution is opposed "because it is contrary to the belief of some that the Book of Genesis must be the exclusive source of doctrine as to the origin of man."

MCLEAN V. ARKANSAS, A 1982 UNITED STATES DISTRICT COURT OPINION

This was a test of the balanced treatment approach proposed by some creationists who recognized after *Epperson* that Darwinian science could not be kept out of the schools. If evolution could not be defeated, the argument went, at least it could be balanced with a science compatible with Genesis. With the encouragement of the Institute for Creation Research, the Arkansas legislature passed a law that required both "creation science" and "evolution science" to be taught in public schools. In wording that reflects a Young Earth Creationist view, the law defined creation science as finding "scientific evidences" that (quoting from the law) include

- sudden creation of the universe, energy, and life from nothing;
- the insufficiency of mutation and natural selection in bringing about the development of all living kinds from a single organism;
- changes only within fixed limits of originally created kinds of plants and animals;
- separate ancestry for man and apes;
- explanation of the earth's geology by catastrophism, including the occurrence of a worldwide flood; and
- a relatively recent inception of the earth and living kinds.

A number of leaders from mainline churches went on record opposing the law (the McLean who gave his name to the
case was a clergyman who headed the Presbyterian Church in
Arkansas). Judge William R. Overton ruled that the law was
an attempt by the state to promote the creation story from Genesis as interpreted from a fundamentalist perspective. Balanced
treatment was thus ruled an unconstitutional attempt to gain
support for a particular religious view, as prohibited by the
First Amendment.

An analysis of the trial by one who testified may be read
in Langdon Gilkey, *Creationism on Trial: Evolution and God at
Little Rock* (Charlottesville: University Press of Virginia, 1985).
The law is printed on page 260.

EDWARDS V. AGUILLARD, A 1987 UNITED STATES SUPREME COURT OPINION

States other than Arkansas passed balanced treatment laws,
and the one from Louisiana ended up in the United States Supreme Court. The law did not define creation science as the
Arkansas law did, with supporters hoping thereby to avoid
direct or indirect reference to Genesis. Nonetheless, the court
ruled seven to two that the law's prescription that if evolution science is taught then creation science must also be taught
was a violation of the constitutional separation of state and
religion.

Justice William J. Brennan wrote for the majority that the
purpose of the law "was clearly to advance the religious viewpoint that a supernatural being created humankind."

He further noted that the law reflected a "fundamentalist
religious fervor" that opposed evolution and that it advanced
"a particular interpretation of the Book of Genesis by a par-

ticular religious group." In response to the claim that creation science can stand alone as a science apart from any religious ties, the opinion notes that in a survey of Louisiana school superintendents in charge of implementing the law, a large proportion interpreted creation science to mean a literal interpretation of Genesis.

KITZMILLER V. DOVER AREA SCHOOL DISTRICT, A 2005 UNITED STATES DISTRICT COURT OPINION

With the failure to get creation science into the public schools, many creationists turned their support toward a new idea, Intelligent Design, as a way to undercut the dominance of Darwinism in the public schools. The board of the Dover Area School District in Pennsylvania, with support from the Discovery Institute (chief voice for ID), voted to require that a statement be read in biology classes that included the following:

> Because Darwin's Theory is a theory, it continues to be tested as new evidence is discovered. The Theory is not a fact. Gaps in the Theory exist for which there is no evidence. A theory is defined as a well-tested explanation that unifies a broad range of observations.
>
> Intelligent Design is an explanation of the origin of life that differs from Darwin's view. The reference book, *Of Pandas and People*, is available for students who might be interested in gaining an understanding of what Intelligent Design actually involves.

A challenge to the board policy was brought by a group of parents in the school district. At the trial supporters of ID attempted to distance themselves from creationism. They argued that, yes, they did presuppose an intelligence outside the natural process but that their view finds support in a number of philosophies and religions and is not coupled with the God of Genesis. They argued that Darwinism is an inadequate explanation of the natural processes and that ID is an alternative scientific view supported by established scientists.

Judge John E. Jones III ruled that ID is not a scientific theory but an old religious idea. He found it to be a form of creationism. In his opinion, he noted the history of fundamentalism and its opposition to Darwinism and put ID in that tradition. Citing *Epperson* and *Edwards*, he judged ID to be an attempt by the school board to introduce the God of Genesis into biology classes and thus was a violation of the First Amendment's prohibition of state sponsorship of religion.[1]

There was no appeal because the members of the school board who established the policy were not reelected and the new board opposed the ID policy.

NOTES

PREFACE

1. Harlow Shapley, ed., *Science Ponders Religion* (New York: Appleton-Century-Crofts, 1960), vii. Quote from preface by Shapley.

CHAPTER 1

1. Harold Bloom, *The Book of J* (New York: Grove Weidenfeld, 1990), 282.
2. Mark 12:26; Rom 10:5; and elsewhere.
3. For dates, see Norman K. Gottwald, *The Hebrew Bible* (Minneapolis: Fortress Press, 1985), 137, 139. As Gottwald points out, there is some disagreement and considerable ongoing discussion about the dating of J and P.
4. Female authorship is supported by Bloom, as we shall see, and also, by Richard Elliott Friedman in *Who Wrote the Bible?* (Englewood Cliffs: Prentice Hall, 1987), 86.
5. The original Hebrew had no vowels, and YHWH is the Roman alphabet equivalent of the Hebrew consonants. The Yahwist story is called J and not Y because the holy name is written *Jahwe* in German, and German scholars first named the document J.

6. Meaning "Four Letters," the Hebrew consonants that are the holy name. According to Exodus 3:15, the name came from Yahweh himself, who gave the name to Moses in the burning bush experience.

7. The Hebrew word *ruach* is translated "wind" or "spirit" or "breath."

8. A helpful analysis of the flood stories is found in Friedman, *Who Wrote the Bible?* 237.

9. Charles H. Long, *Alpha: The Myths of Creation* (New York: Collier, 1963), contains a number of myths with preexisting water. Alexander Heidel, *The Babylonian Genesis* (Chicago: University of Chicago Press, 1942), tells the Marduk story.

10. *Creatio ex nihilo* is rejected in process theology, as seen in the writings of John B. Cobb Jr. and Alfred North Whitehead, and by many feminists, such as Sally McFague in our next chapter. It is defended by some, including Jurgen Moltmann, *God in Creation* (Minneapolis: Fortress Press, 1993), 74.

11. Asherah is singular, Asheroth plural.

12. An analysis of the religious pluralism in the land is Morton Smith, *Palestinian Parties and Politics That Shaped the Old Testament* (New York: Columbia University Press, 1971), 15–17. Smith notes that marriage with aliens was accepted during the time of David and Solomon but was later opposed because of concerns about the other gods that this involved.

13. There were other gods and goddesses, sometimes with counterparts in Mosopotamia or Egypt. Local variations had different names. Numerous small clay figurines apparently representing fertility goddesses have been found in archaeological digs in Palestine, so many that tourists may purchase them in antiquities shops in Jerusalem. They probably were of some comfort to women in childbearing. In addition to Smith, see Raphael Patai, *The Hebrew Goddess* (Jersey City: KTAV, 1967).

14. 2 Kings 23:6.

15. Although this claim may be supported, it should be recognized as a generalization. Some biblical passages see Yahweh associated with nature, and some of the neighboring gods were concerned with history and politics.

16. Later in the Hebrew Bible there are references to the womb of God, as will be seen in chapter 2.

17. For Christians, chapter 1 of the Gospel of John restates Genesis 1 in saying, "In the beginning was the Word," and then goes on to identify the Christ with the action of God in Genesis 1.

18. This emphasis on the power of words is found elsewhere in the ancient Middle East, especially in Egypt, as noted by Claus Westermann, *Genesis 1–11: A Commentary*, trans. John J. Scullion (Minneapolis: Augsburg, 1984), 40. Outside Israel the use of words involved magic (correct recitation produced magical results), notes Nahum M. Sarna, *Understanding Genesis* (New York: Shocken, 1966), 12. In China the Confucian tradition focused on words and the need to find words that reflect the nature of ultimate reality.

19. Plato, *Symposium*, trans. Benjamin Jowett (Indianapolis: Bobbs-Merrill, 1956), 30.

20. June Singer, *Androgyny: Toward a New Theory of Sexuality* (Garden City: Doubleday, 1976), 88. Singer thinks the Priestly story relates "image of God" to "male and female" and thus understands God as androgynous (a claim few others would support). Also, some medieval rabbis speculated that the man and woman were back-to-back and double-faced and androgynous until split, as noted in Kristen Kvam et al., eds., *Eve and Adam: Jewish, Christian and Muslim Readings on Genesis and Gender* (Bloomington: Indiana University Press, 1999), 77.

21. This is the view of Gottlieb, *Hebrew Bible*, 329. Phyllis Trible first argued for androgyny in J but then changed her view to see a "sexually undifferentiated creature" who became male and female when the rib was removed. Trible, "Not a Jot, Not a Tittle: Genesis 2–3 after Twenty Years," in Kvam et al. *Eve and Adam*, 440.

22. For an overview, see Elaine Pagels, *Adam, Eve, and the Serpent* (New York: Random House, 1988).

23. Strong critical rejection of Augustine may be found in Pagels and in Uta Ranke-Heinemann, *Eunuchs for the Kingdom of God: Woman, Sexuality and the Catholic Church*, transl. Peter Heinegg (New York: Penguin, 1991).

24. Augustine speculated that the first pair could have had sex without desire, a kind of spiritual sex, to produce children.

25. Augustine, *The City of God against the Pagans*, trans. Philip Levine (Cambridge: Harvard University Press, 1958). "What already existed was the seminal substance from which we were to be generated. Obviously, when this substance was debased through sin and shackled with the bond of death in just condemnation, no man could be born in any other condition." Book 13, chapter 14. Following Augustine, Roman Catholic tradition has said that Adam, Eve, and Jesus were the only humans not produced through semen, so they were produced sinless. The later teaching of the Immaculate Conception says Mary also was born sinless because a miracle occurred when her mother conceived.

26. Michael Gold, *Does God Belong in the Bedroom?* (Philadelphia: Jewish Publication Society, 1992), 6, 14, 31.

27. Westermann, *Genesis 1–11*, 116–17.

28. Ibid., 115. A third level was later added to make three levels—heaven above, earth, and *sheol* (or hell) below.

29. Helpful in distinguishing the various critical approaches is Carl R. Holladay, "Contemporary Methods of Reading the Bible," in *The New Interpreter's Bible* (Nashville: Abingdon, 1994), 1:125.

30. This is not to say that all this was new in the eighteenth century, for there were prominent scholars in earlier centuries (for example, Origen, Augustine, and Luther) who approached the Bible critically, and before the Enlightenment a growing sensitivity to the historical background of the Bible was seen in the Renaissance.

31. Feminist biblical scholars usually accept the historical-critical method, but with reservations. They say feminists should look out for male biases in the approach and disagree with scholars who say the method should be impartial and objective. For many feminists, biblical scholarship should not be impartial but should aim at liberating women and other oppressed groups. Elizabeth Schüssler Fiorenza, "Remembering the Past in Creating the Future: Historical-Critical Scholarship and Feminist Biblical Interpretation," in Adela Yarbro Collins, ed., *Feminist Perspectives on Biblical Scholarship* (Chico: Scholars, 1985), 55–56.

32. Phyllis Trible, *God and the Rhetoric of Sexuality* (Philadelphia: Fortress Press, 1978), 8.

33. The term comes from Holladay, who compares the "Divine Oracle Paradigm" with the "Historical Paradigm" of biblical criticism.

34. Helpful is Marcus J. Borg, *The Heart of Christianity* (New York: HarperSanFrancisco, 2003), chapter 3. Borg avoids "conservative" and "liberal" and instead compares the "earlier paradigm" (what we have called "divine oracle") with an "emerging paradigm" that focuses on the human and the historical in interpreting the Bible.

35. Darrell Jodock comments, "No contemporary theory of the authority of the Bible can assume that a person will be convinced of the Bible's authority apart from participation in the community of faith." Jodock, *The Church's Bible: Its Contemporary Authority* (Minneapolis: Fortress Press, 1989), 74.

36. Elizabeth Schüssler Fiorenza prefers not to speak of biblical texts as inspired because they are the products of communities and represent political interests, especially those of males. Yet she says the Bible "can become holy scripture for women-church" where women and men support each other in a community of faith. Schüssler Fiorenza, "The Will to Choose or to Reject: Continuing Our Critical Work," in Letty Russell, ed., *Feminist Interpretation of the Bible* (Philadelphia: Westminster, 1985), 136. Letty Russell says for feminists "the word of God is not identical with the biblical texts" but leaves room for authority growing out of the process by which a community deals with the texts. Russell, "Introduction: Liberating the Word," in Russell, *Feminist Interpretation*, 17. Rosemary Radford Ruether argues for a "method of correlation" by which both Bible and women's experiences bring something to interpreting the Bible. Ruether, "Feminist Interpretation: A Method of Correlation," in Russell, *Feminist Interpretation*.

37. Some fundamentalists have said the Bible is without error as originally given. As it has been copied through the ages, some errors have slipped in. Thus "lower criticism" that focuses on discerning the accuracy of the text is accepted, but "higher criticism" (most of biblical criticism) is not. James Barr, *Fundamentalism* (Philadelphia: Westminster, 1977), 279.

38. Many Americans have high regard for the Bible but do not accept it literally. The 2006 Gallup poll found 49 percent saying, "The

Bible is the inspired word of God but not everything in it is to be taken literally." For Gallup data, see Frank Newport, "Twenty-eight Percent Believe Bible Is Actual Word of God," in *The Gallup Poll Briefing* (May 2006), and George Gallup Jr. and Jim Castelli, *The People's Religion: American Faith in the '90s* (New York: Macmillan, 1989), 61. A 2004 poll by the Pew Forum found a similar result: 35 percent said everything in the Bible is literally true, while 43 percent said the Bible is the word of God but not everything in it should be taken literally. http://www.pewforum .org/docs.

39. This change will be considered in chapter 4.
40. Statistics are from *The Yearbook of American and Canadian Churches* (Nashville: Abingdon, 2005).

Protestant denominations usually classed mainline
(members, all 2005):

United Methodist Church	8,251,000
Evangelical Lutheran Church in America	5,038,000
Presbyterian Church (USA)	3,241,000
Episcopal Church	2,320,000
American Baptist Churches	1,433,000
United Church of Christ	1,297,000

Protestant denominations usually classed fundamentalist
(members, all 2005):

Southern Baptist Convention	16,000,000
Lutheran Church—Missouri Synod	2,489,000

The Roman Catholic Church	67,260,000

41. Gerald P. Fogarty, "Dissent at Catholic University: The Case of Henry Poels," *America* 155, no. 9 (October 11, 1986). Poels saw his position supported before his death in 1948.
42. Raymond E. Brown et al., eds., *The Jerome Bible Commentary* (Englewood Cliffs: Prentice-Hall, 1968), xvii, 3.
43. An example is Richard Elliott Friedman, whom we have cited earlier in this chapter.

44. British Rabbi Louis Jacobs, who died in 2006, was widely recognized as a brilliant scholar and thought by some to be the greatest British Jew. Yet he was never totally accepted by the Orthodox Jewish establishment because he said the Torah was not written by Moses but was the product of many hands. Obituary in the *New York Times*, July 9, 2006.

CHAPTER 2

1. Theodor Reik, *The Creation of Woman* (New York: Geoge Braziller, 1960), 12.
2. Elizabeth Cady Stanton, ed., *The Woman's Bible* (New York: European Publishing, 1898), 20. The argument that Genesis 1 presents a heavenly Mother receives almost no support today.
3. Ibid., 20–27.
4. This chapter deals with Jewish and Christian feminists who want to reform their traditions. As noted in the preface, there are others who reject *all* the Bible and its religions as hopelessly negative toward women and who think the idea of reforming the traditions is wishful thinking. For example, former Roman Catholic Mary Daly in *Beyond God the Father* (Boston: Beacon, 1973) said a depatriarchalized Bible might have enough material worth saving to print in a small pamphlet (206). Secularists Simone de Beauvoir (*The Second Sex*, 1952) and Kate Millett (*Sexual Politics*, 1969) were very negative toward the Yahwist story.
5. Letty M. Russell, "Authority and the Challenge of Feminist Interpretation," in Russell, ed., *Feminist Interpretation of the Bible* (Philadelphia: Westminster, 1985), 141. Phyllis Trible shows how dangerous the Bible may be for women in her analysis of the tragic stories of four biblical women in *Texts of Terror: Literary-Feminist Readings of Biblical Narratives* (Philadelphia: Fortress Press, 1984).
6. Phyllis Trible, "Depatriarchalizing in Biblical Interpretation," *Journal of the American Academy of Religion* 16, no. 1 (March 1973): 31.
7. Hermeneutics "studies the theoretical issues involved in getting a text from one time and place to have meaning for, or speak

to a person in, another time and place." Darrell Jodock, *The Church's Bible: Its Contemporary Authority* (Minneapolis: Fortress Press, 1989), 157. It may be compared to exegesis, which is interpretation.

8. Elisabeth Schüssler Fiorenza, "Transforming the Legacy of *The Woman's Bible*," in Schüssler Fiorenza, ed., *Searching the Scriptures: A Feminist Introduction* (New York: Crossroad, 1993), 11.

9. Phyllis Trible, "Postscript," in Russell, *Feminist Interpretation*, 149.

10. Ruether, "Feminist Interpretation: A Method of Correlation," in Russell, *Feminist Interpretation*, 114–15. Elizabeth A. Johnson speaks of reading the Bible through the "lens of women's flourishing" in *She Who Is: The Mystery of God in Feminist Theological Discourse* (New York: Crossroad, 1992), 17. This is not to say that women's experience is more important than men's, for many feminists are willing to balance the focus on women with a reformulated emphasis on men's experience, as we will see with Sallie McFague later in this chapter.

11. The influence of this passage has faded in most Christian groups. For those of us who remember the fifties, before feminist views began to gain traction, there is the vivid memory of all those colorful hats women wore to church and of the millenary shops that did a thriving business in supporting Paul's advice.

12. From Kristen Kvam et al., eds., *Eve and Adam: Jewish, Christian and Muslim Readings on Genesis and Gender* (Bloomington: Indiana University Press, 1999), 132.

13. Ibid., 227.

14. From Elizabeth A. Clark and Herbert Richardson, eds., *Woman and Religion: The Original Sourcebook of Women in Christian Thought* (New York: HarperSanFrancisco, 1996), 163.

15. Ibid., 126. The Latin title *Malleus Maleficarum* means "a hammer against witches."

16. Examples may be found in chapter 2 of Kvam et al., *Eve and Adam*.

17. Sirach (also called the Wisdom of Ben Sira) 25:24, using the NRSV.

18. Printed in Kvam et al., *Eve and Adam*, 65.

19. Rosemary Radford Ruether is an example of feminist rejection

of the Yahwist story, as she argues, "The story reflects the final stage of the male puberty drama, where woman as mother is not only overthrown but disappears, and woman as wife is 'created' as a secondary being, adjunct to her husband." Ruether, *Gaia and God: An Ecofeminist Theology of Earth Healing* (New York: HarperSanFrancisco, 1992), 179.

20. Kvam et al., *Eve and Adam*, 204.

21. Judith Plaskow, "The Coming of Lilith: Toward a Feminist Theology," in Carol P. Christ and Judith Plaskow, eds., *Womanspirit Rising: A Feminist Reader in Religion* (New York: Harper & Row, 1979).

22. Judith Plaskow, "Lilith Revisited," in Kvam et al., *Eve and Adam*, 427–29.

23. Ibid., 428.

24. Trible taught biblical studies at Union Theological Seminary, connected to Columbia University in New York, among other places. Bloom was a fixture at Yale University and also taught elsewhere. Both are now retired.

25. Phyllis Trible, "Eve and Adam: Genesis 2–3 Reread," in Christ and Plaskow, *Womanspirit Rising*, 74.

26. Phyllis Trible, "Not a Jot, Not a Tittle: Genesis 2–3 after Twenty Years," in Kvam et al. *Eve and Adam*," 440.

27. Phyllis Trible, "Eve and Miriam: From the Margins to the Center," in Hershel Shanks, ed., *Feminist Approaches to the Bible* (Washington: Biblical Archaeology Society, 1995), 15.

28. Harold Bloom, *The Book of J* (New York: Grove Weidenfeld, 1990). The book includes a new translation of the Yahwist account by David Rosenberg and an interpretation by Bloom.

29. Ibid., 26.

30. Ibid., 180, 183, 284.

31. John Barton has an insightful review in *The New York Review of Books* 37, no. 18 (November 22, 1990), in which he says of *The Book of J*, "It may be brilliant, or it may be wildly anachronistic—I suspect it is both—but it is not a book one can ignore."

32. Phyllis Trible notes, "Feminism has no difficulty making a case against the Bible. It has no difficulty convicting the Bible of patriarchy. One could say this recognition is the *sine qua non* of feminist readings of the Bible." Trible, "Eve and Miriam," 7.

33. An interesting exception is Matthew 1, where Joseph is listed in the genealogy but Mary (a virgin) is recognized as the mother of Jesus.

34. Daly, *Beyond God the Father*, 19. Few feminists would go the next step with Daly to say that the Supreme Phallus must be cut off.

35. Ruether often argues feminists should blame Greek thought as much as the Bible for Western bias against women. Rosemary Radford Ruether, *Sexism and God-Talk: Toward a Feminist Theology* (Boston: Beacon, 1983), 78.

36. Ruether writes, "God is both male and female and neither male nor female. One needs inclusive language for God that draws on the image of both genders." Ibid., 67. She suggests the term "God/ess" as a solution that includes male and female.

37. Phyllis Trible in detail analyzes the metaphor of God's womb in the Hebrew Bible in *God and the Rhetoric of Sexuality* (Philadelphia: Fortress Press, 1978), chap. 2.

38. Carol Meyers, "Female Images of God in the Hebrew Bible," in Meyers, ed., *Women in Scripture: A Dictionary* (New York: Houghton Mifflin, 2000).

39. A testimony to once-powerful female images are two books of scripture: the biblical Song of Solomon (with gender mutuality and association of the female with power) and the apocryphal Wisdom of Solomon (with its praise of female wisdom as a manifestation of God).

40. Elizabeth A. Johnson, *She Who Is: The Mystery of God in Feminist Theological Discourse* (New York: Crossroad, 1992), 134.

41. Sallie McFague, *Models of God: Theology for an Ecological, Nuclear Age* (Philadelphia: Fortress Press, 1987). This book was awarded the American Academy of Religion Award for Excellence in 1998, showing McFague's respect in the larger academic community. While our focus will be on McFague, there are others who advocate female images. Rosemary Radford Ruether says, "We can speak of the root human image of the divine as the Primal Matrix, the great womb within which all things, gods and humans, sky and earth, human and nonhuman beings, are generated." Ruether, *Sexism and God-Talk*, 48.

42. McFague, *Models*, xi.

43. Sallie McFague, *Metaphorical Theology: Models of God in Religious Language* (Philadelphia: Fortress Press, 1982), 145.

44. McFague is critical of the common model of God as monarch. She notes that people often sing the popular "Hallelujah Chorus" of Handel's *Messiah* without recognizing its image of God is "dangerous." The soaring music presents "an asymmetrical dualism" between God and world, with God and world only distantly related. McFague, *Models*, 64.

45. Ibid., 106.

46. Ibid., 99.

47. This reading of Genesis 1 does not come from McFague but is consistent with her writings.

48. Ibid., 109.

49. Sallie McFague, *The Body of God: An Ecological Theology* (Minneapolis: Fortress Press, 1993), 39. Ruether, *Gaia and God*, 40.

50. Evangelicals are those who have had a personal inward experience of Christ and often speak of being "born again." They tend to be conservative in personal lifestyle, religion, and social outlook. Fundamentalists, as we noted in chapter 1, read the Bible literally and think of it as infallible. Some evangelicals are fundamentalists, but some are not.

51. From their website, http://www cbeinternational.org, and from Gilbert Bilezikian, *Beyond Sex Roles: A Guide for the Study of Female Roles in the Bible* (Grand Rapids: Baker, 1985).

52. Points here are drawn from their website, http://www.cbmw. org, and from Wayne Gruden, *Evangelical Feminism and Biblical Truth* (Sisters, Ore.: Multnomah, 2004).

53. Quote from Susan T. Foh, "The Head of the Woman Is the Man," in Kvam et al., *Eve and Adam*, 392.

54. Gruden, *Evangelical Feminism*, 109.

55. Ibid., 51.

CHAPTER 3

1. From an address reprinted in Roger S. Gottlieb, ed., *This Sacred Earth: Religion, Nature, Environment* (New York: Routledge, 2004), 227. The Patriarch is Archbishop of Constantinople and is sometimes called "the green Patriarch."

2. "The Historical Roots of Our Ecological Crisis," *Science* 155, no. 3767 (March 10, 1967). White was not the only one to make such a claim, although his article has received much of the attention.

Arnold Toynbee advanced the argument in "The Religious Background of the Present Environmental Crisis," in David and Eileen Spring, eds., *Ecology and Religion in History* (New York: Harper & Row, 1974). Toynbee wrote, "For people who have been brought up in the monotheist tradition, it is difficult to re-gain the awe of nature that was shattered by the pronouncement in Genesis i, 28" (147).

3. Again, note that this is a debate *within* Judaism and Christianity. Lynn White was a Christian and churchman and wanted to see Christianity reformed to take seriously its own tradition of St. Francis. See Thomas S. Derr, *Environmental Ethics and Christian Humanism* (Nashville: Abingdon, 1996), 19.

4. William P. Brown, *The Ethos of the Cosmos* (Grand Rapids: Eerdmans, 1999), 44. Jeremy Cohen, *"Be Fertile and Increase, Fill the Earth and Master It": The Ancient and Medieval Career of a Biblical Text* (Ithaca, N.Y.: Cornell University Press, 1989), 16.

5. Barry Commoner, quoted in Douglas John Hall, *The Steward* (Eugene, Ore.: Wipf & Stock, 1990), 142.

6. Quoted in Larry L. Rasmussen, *Earth Community, Earth Ethics* (Maryknoll, N.Y.: Orbis, 1998), 229–30.

7. Cited in Roderick F. Nash, *The Rights of Nature* (Madison: University of Wisconsin Press, 1989), 120.

8. In a 2004 statement on radio, cited in Heather Eaton, *Introducing Ecofeminist Theologies* (London: T&T Clark, 2005), 96.

9. An introduction is Vine Deloria, *God is Red* (Golden, Colo.: Fulcrum, 2003).

10. Jewish writers focus on the covenant in the stories, for example, Bradley Shavit Artson, "Our Covenant with Stones," in Martin D. Yaffe, ed., *Judaism and Environmental Ethics* (Lanham, Md.: Lexington, 2001). For a Christian, see James A. Nash, *Loving Nature* (Nashville: Abingdon, 1991), 100.

11. Phyllis Trible, *God and the Rhetoric of Sexuality* (Philadelphia: Fortress Press, 1978), 78.

12. Steven Bouma-Prediger, "Living on the Land, Living a Christian Land Ethic," *Creation Care Magazine* (Summer 2003), available at http://www.creationcare.org.

13. Brown, *Ethos of the Cosmos*, 138. A detailed discussion of *'adam* from *'adama* is found in this book and in Theodore Hiebert, *The*

Yahwist Landscape: Nature and Religion in Early Israel (New York: Oxford University Press, 1996), 35.

14. Further, for the Yahwist, the naming of the animals by *'adam* may be understood as a reflection of human life among the animals and not as a statement of superiority, as some critics say. H. Paul Santmire argues that the creator withdraws "to encourage creaturely bonding . . . Comradeship on the part of Adam with the animals seems to be implied in this naming scene, perhaps even with nuances of friendship and self-giving." Santmire, *Nature Reborn: The Ecological and Cosmic Promise of Christian Theology* (Minneapolis: Fortress Press, 2000), 40.

15. Cohen, *"Be Fertile and Increase . . ."* 6.

16. Jewish scholars have taken up Lynn White's challenge, but the near consensus is that the problem lies more with Christianity than with Judaism. Some say the issue is not the "Judeo-Christian" tradition but the "Greco-Christian." See Jeanne Kay, "Concepts of Nature in the Hebrew Bible," in Yaffe, *Judaism and Environmental Ethics*, 87.

17. Walter Brueggemann, *The Land* (Minneapolis: Fortress Press, 2002), 2.

18. Reading Leopold with the eyes of a Christian is Bouma-Prediger, "Living on the Land."

19. Jeremy Cohen has done an exhaustive study of Gen 1:28, including how it has been interpreted through the centuries. He concludes that the modern sense of "have dominion" (he translates it "master it") as unrestrained human control was never part of historical understandings. Cohen, *"Be Fertile and Increase . . ."* 5.

20. Genesis 1:29-30 and 9:1-7.

21. The Christian Vegetarian Association has a website, as does Jewish Vegetarians of North America.

22. Leviticus 25:3-7.

23. Eilon Schwartz, *"Bal Tashcit*: A Jewish Environmental Precept," in Yaffe, ed.

24. Seth Zuckerman, "Redwood Rabbis," *Sierra Magazine* 83, no. 6 (November 1998).

25. Hall, *The Steward*, 240, quotes Jeremy Rifkin, "The new concept is that dominion is stewardship rather than ownership and conservation rather than exploitation" Further, "What is the real,

orthodox Christian attitude toward nature? It is, in a word, stewardship," writes Thomas Derr, *Environmental Ethics*, 22.

26. Cited by Rasmussen, *Earth Community*, 103.

27. Hall, *The Steward*, 40–41.

28. David Ehrenfeld and Philip J. Bentley, "Judaism and the Practice of Stewardship," in Yaffe, *Judaism and Environmental Ethics*.

29. Hall in *The Steward* speaks of the "ecclesiastical captivity of the symbol," 101.

30. Hart, *Sacramental Commons: Christian Ecological Ethics* (Lanham, Md.: Rowman & Littlefield, 2006), 120.

31. Joining Hart in criticizing stewardship are Paul Santmire, *Nature Reborn*, 120; Larry Rasmussen, *Earth Community*, 230; John F. Haught, "Christianity and Ecology," in Gottlieb, *This Sacred Earth*, 239; and Elizabeth Dodson Gray, *Green Paradise Lost* (Wellesley, Mass.: Roundtable, 1981), 20.

32. Advancing this interpretation were influential scholars such as Gerhard von Rad, G. Ernest Wright, and H. A. Frankfort. Hiebert argues that these scholars got it wrong, that the Yahwist does *not* make a radical separation of nature from history but in fact is very positive toward nature. Hiebert, *Yahwist Landscape*, 4–8.

33. Much of liberation theology has greened with a developed sensitivity to the natural world. A leading third-world theologian is Leonard Boff, who ties human liberation to nature-sensitivity in *Ecology and Liberation* (Maryknoll, N.Y.: Orbis, 1995). We will see the greening of feminist theology in the next section.

34. *The Greening of Theology* is the title of a book by Steven Bouma-Prediger (Atlanta: Scholars, 1995). Paradigm shift, ellipse, and triangle are from Santmire, *Nature Reborn*, 13.

35. Nash, *Loving Nature*, 139. Nash notes that he is in "virgin territory" in talking of a Christian's love of nature.

36. "When Clear Air Is a Biblical Obligation" and "Evangelical Leaders Join Global Warming Initiative," *New York Times*, November 7, 2005, and February 8, 2006. See also http:// creationcare.org.

37. Many who champion a green outlook would *not* want to be identified as panentheists. This would include James A. Nash, H. Paul Santmire, Ted Peters, and Thomas S. Derr.

38. Here we draw in part from the eight themes of panentheism listed

by Michael W. Brierley, "Naming a Quiet Revolution: The Panentheistic Turn in Modern Theology," in Philip Clayton and Arthur Peacocke, eds., *In Whom We Live and Move and Have Our Being: Panentheistic Reflections on God's Presence in a Scientific World* (Grand Rapids: Eerdmans, 2004), 3–10. Brierley notes 34 authors who consider themselves panentheists, a list that includes (in addition to Clayton and Peacocke) Jurgen Moltmann, Leonardo Boff, Marcus Borg, John Cobb, Schubert Ogden, John Macquarrie, and Kallistos Ware. Included also are feminist thinkers Rosemary Radford Ruether and Sallie McFague.

39. Philip Clayton calls this the "panentheistic analogy." Clayton, "Panentheism in Metaphysical and Scientific Perspective," in Clayton and Peacocke, *In Whom We Live*, 83.

40. David Tracy says a positive contribution of panentheism is a recognition of "God's radically relational nature" and the "intrinsically relational character of all reality." Tracy, *On Naming the Present: God, Hermeneutics, and Church* (Maryknoll, N.Y.: Orbis, 1994), 37, 41.

41. Acts 17:28. Note that this is the title of the book edited by Clayton and Peacocke.

42. Argued by Philip Clayton, *God and Contemporary Science* (Grand Rapids: Eerdmans, 1997), 102–4, and others.

43. Peacocke, "Articulating God's Presence in and to the World Unveiled by the Sciences," in Clayton and Peacocke, *In Whom We Live*, 154.

44. Ware, "God Immanent yet Transcendent," in Clayton and Peacock, *In Whom We Live*, 159.

45. For a discussion of God's energy, see John Meyendorff, *Byzantine Theology: Historical Trends and Doctrinal Themes* (New York: Fordham University Press, 1974), 185–88.

46. Colossians 1:15-20. Joseph Sittler used this passage as the basis for his 1961 speech at a World Council of Churches meeting in New Delhi, a speech proclaiming a cosmic Christ and making Sittler an early spokesperson for green theology. A Lutheran, Sittler had great respect for Orthodox views of the natural world. Sittler, "Called to Unity," in Sittler, *Evocations of Grace: Writings on Ecology, Theology and Ethics*, ed. Steven Bouma-Prediger and Peter Bakken (Grand Rapids: Eerdmans, 2000).

47. Pierre Teilhard de Chardin, *Hymn of the Universe* (New York: Harper & Row, 1961), 17.

48. Matthew Fox, *Confessions: The Making of a Post-Denominational Priest* (San Francisco: HarperCollins, 1996), and Fox, *The Coming of the Cosmic Christ* (New York: HarperCollins, 1988). Fox was a Dominican priest and is now an Anglican priest. Masses of this type are likely to depend not on the first chapter of Genesis but on the creation story in the first chapter of John with its christo-centric view of the universe. "In the beginning was the Word . . . All things came into being through him, and without him not one thing came into being" (John 1:1, 3).

49. Rosemary Radford Ruether, *Sexism and God-Talk: Toward a Feminist Theology* (Boston: Beacon, 1983), 73.

50. Lovelock, *The Ages of Gaia: A Biography of Our Living Earth* (New York: W. W. Norton, 1988), xiii–xix.

51. Rosemary Radford Ruether, *Gaia and God: An Ecofeminist Theology of Earth Healing* (New York: HarperSanFrancisco, 1992), 254.

52. Ivone Gebara, *Longing for Running Water: Ecofeminism and Liberation* (Minneapolis: Fortress Press, 1999), vii.

53. Thomas Berry with physicist Brian Swimme, *The Universe Story* (New York: HarperSanFrancisco, 1992), 7.

54. Theodore Hiebert argues that Berry's view of the Bible is based on the now outdated interpretation by important biblical scholars of the previous generation that the Bible is concerned with history and is negative toward nature. Hiebart, *Yahwist Landscape*, 14.

55. Chapter 10, "The New Story," in Thomas Berry, *The Dream of the Earth* (San Francisco: Sierra Club, 1990). Sallie McFague also celebrates "the new creation story," *The Body of God: An Ecological Theology* (Minneapolis: Fortress Press, 1993), 39, as does Larry Rasmussen, *Earth Community*, 266. The description of earth as Gaia is an old story made new in the retelling.

56. Karl Rahner, *On the Theology of Death*, trans. Charles H. Henkey (New York: Herder & Herder, 1961), 25–31.

57. Watt was an official in the Reagan administration. In 2005 he rejected the claim that he is not concerned for the environment in a spirited written exchange with Duane Larson, president of Wartburg Theological Seminary. *Dialog* 44, no. 4 (Winter 2005).

58. "Preserving and Cherishing the Earth," *American Journal of Physics* 58, no. 7 (July 1990).

CHAPTER 4

1. Scribbled in a notebook by Darwin, cited in Jonathan Weiner, *The Beak of a Finch* (New York: Alfred A. Knopf, 1995), 281

2. http://www.bryan.edu.

3. William Safire, "Neo-Creo," *New York Times Magazine* (August 21, 2005). The term has a different history and meaning in Roman Catholic tradition, where creationism means God creates a soul that is inserted into each new body produced by biological parents. Creationism is contrasted with traducianism, which understands the human soul as being passed along from the two parents.

4. James Ussher, *The Annals of the World* (Green Forest, Ark.: Master, 2003), an updating by Larry and Marion Pierce of the original 1658 edition, 17.

5. Thomas Robinson, *The Bible Timeline* (New York: Barnes & Noble Books, 1992), offers 3941 BCE as a possible date for creation.

6. Darrell Jodock, *The Church's Bible: Its Contemporary Authority* (Minneapolis: Fortress Press, 1989), 52.

7. C. I. Scofield, ed., *The Scofield Reference Bible* (New York: Oxford University Press, 1917), 3. Scofield says the earth in its geology "bears everywhere the marks of such a catastrophe."

8. Jeremiah 4, Ezekiel 28, and Isaiah 14 are cited as showing this rebellion and punishment.

9. George M. Marsden, *Understanding Fundamentalism and Evangelicalism* (Grand Rapids: Eerdmans, 1991), 129.

10. "Concordism" describes attempts to find parallels between what science says and what Genesis says, thus avoiding conflict. At one time popular, this has been abandoned today by most Jews and Christians, except in creationist circles.

11. Marsden, *Understanding Fundamentalism and Evangelicalism*, 129, 165, 173.

12. Today's biology adds to Darwin's ideas knowledge about genetics (especially about DNA) unknown in his day. Just as there is random variation in the environment, there also is variation in

the passing of the genetic code, with even small variations having major consequences over time. With this synthesis of Darwin and genetics, biologists today are neo-Darwinists, although most are still called Darwinists.

13. Ian G. Barbour, *Religion in an Age of Science* (New York: Harper-SanFrancisco, 1990), 220. For a comparison of Newtonian and twentieth-century science, see 219–21.

14. Ronald L. Numbers, *The Creationists* (New York: Alfred A. Knopf, 1992), 299. Numbers in several books is the chief chronicler of creationism. Whitcomb (a theology professor) is listed as coeditor of *The Genesis Flood*, but it was Morris (with a Ph.D. from the University of Minnesota in hydraulic engineering) who became the most influential spokesman for modern creationism. Morris died in 2006 and was given a lengthy obituary by the *New York Times* (March 4, 2006).

15. Kenneth Miller says this makes God a charlatan, a cruel God who deceives. Miller, *Finding Darwin's God* (New York: Harper & Row, 1999), 80.

16. John C. Morris and Henry M. Morris, *The Genesis Flood: The Biblical Record and Its Scientific Implications* (Philipsburg, N.J.: Presbyterian and Reformed Publishing Co., 1961), 10, 173, 232. The claim about humans and dinosaurs was later halfheartedly retracted. The ICR is convinced that the flood happened as the Bible says and periodically sends teams to Turkey to try to find the ark's remains on a mountaintop. Also Numbers, *The Creationists*, 202.

17. *The Genesis Flood*, 1, and http://www.icr.org.

18. Numbers, *The Creationists*, 102.

19. Care should be taken to avoid overgeneralization. There are some evangelical colleges and seminaries that are Christ-centered and Bible-believing but not creationist, and although conservative in biblical interpretation, they cannot be classed fundamentalist. Calvin College and Fuller Seminary are examples.

20. The Association for Biblical Higher Education (Bible colleges) has 91 members, with an additional 92 listed as affiliates or applicants. See http://www.abhe.gospelcom.net. Almost all Bible colleges are creationist in one form or another. There is an additional group of 102 Christian colleges (not to be confused with church-related colleges) that are Christ-centered but not necessarily fundamen-

talist. Some Christian colleges are creationist (for example, Bryan College), some not (Calvin College). Not on these lists is Jerry Falwell's influential Liberty University, which has a Creation Studies Department and a doctrinal statement that says the Bible is "inerrant in the originals and authoritative in all matters," the "universe was created in six historical days," and Adam was the first human. See http://www.liberty.edu.

21. Henry M. Morris, *The Biblical Basis for Modern Science* (Green Forest, Ark.: Master, 2002), 37, 240.

22. Ibid., 145.

23. Ibid., 111.

24. Ibid., 347.

25. Ibid., 181. Since Adam is so important, it is not surprising to read that God programmed him with a perfect language so he could name the animals and also that "Adam most probably was the author of Genesis 2:4b—5:1," where he was telling us of his experiences. http://www.answersingenesis/creation.org.

26. Duane T. Gish, *Evolution: The Fossils Still Say No* (El Cajon, Calif.: Institute for Creation Research, 1995), 323.

27. Stephen T. Asma, "Dinosaurs on the Ark: The Creation Museum," *Chronicle of Higher Education* 53 (May 18, 2007). Also http://www. answersingenesis.org and http://www.creationmuseum.org.

28. Hugh Ross, *The Genesis Question: Scientific Advances and the Accuracy of Genesis* (Colorado Springs: NavPress, 2001), 19, 29, 86, 108, 115. Also http://www.reasonstobelieve.org/resources.

29. Frank Newport "Almost Half of Americans Believe Humans Did Not Evolve," *The Gallup Poll Briefing* (June 5, 2006). Based on telephone interviews with 2,002 adults in 2004 and 2006. Thirteen percent agreed with a third option, "Human beings developed over millions of years from less advanced forms of life, but God had no part in this process." Inconsistency in the responses is illustrated by the fact that 46 percent agreed with a creationist question here, but only 28 percent agreed with a question that may be identified with fundamentalism (in another Gallup poll the same year, noted in chapter 1).

30. There are noisy exceptions to this irenic picture, particularly in the attacks upon all religion by some scientists, such as Oxford biologist Richard Dawkins.

31. Langdon Gilkey, *Creationism on Trial: Evolution and God at Little Rock* (Charlottesville: University of Virginia Press, 1985), 83, 269.

32. "The Dialogue between Theology and Science," 10, a 1982 statement, http://www.pcusa.org/theologyandworship/science/dialogue.

33. From a 1982 statement titled "Evolution and Creationism," in Molleen Matsumura, ed., *Voices for Evolution* (Berkeley: National Center for Science Education, 1995). The Presbyterian Church (USA) came into being in 1983 when northern and southern branches merged. The two statements quoted here come from earlier bodies but are now officially the view of the Presbyterian Church (USA).

34. "Truth Cannot Contradict Truth," address of Pope John Paul II, October 22, 1996, available at http://www.newadvent.org/library/docs.

35. A study by the church's International Theological Commission, http://www.vatican.va/roman_congregations/cfaith/cti, 69. John L. Allen says that Pope Benedict is very interested in the dialogue between Christianity and science but will be slow to issue a formal statement about evolution. He may have some sympathy for the Intelligent Design view being advanced in America, but his view of how God influences the evolutionary process is different from that usually identified with ID. See Allen's editorial "Benedict's Thinking on Creation and Evolution," in *National Catholic Reporter* 6, no. 1 (September 1, 2006).

36. John F. Haught, *God After Darwin: A Theology of Evolution* (Boulder, Colo.: Westview, 2000), ix, 5, 23.

37. Ibid., 53–56, 112.

38. Ibid., 112. Haught notes that Jurgen Moltmann emphasizes kenotic theology in *God in Creation* (Minneapolis: Fortress Press, 1993), 88. See also John F. Haught, "Darwin, Design and the Promise of Nature," 2004 Boyle Lecture, http://www.stmarylebow.co.uk.

39. John F. Haught, *Responses to 101 Questions on God and Evolution* (New York: Paulist Press, 2001), 27–28.

40. Haught, *God after Darwin*, 16.

41. Haught, *Responses to 101 Questions*, 78, 79.

42. Carl Sagan, *Cosmos* (New York: Random House, 1980), 5.

43. http://www.rac.org/articles.

44. http://www.rabbis.org/news/article.

45. In the 1987 *Edwards v. Aguillard* Supreme Court decision that ruled against creationism, *amici curiae* briefs opposing creationism were filed by the American Jewish Congress, the Anti-Defamation League of B'nai Brith, and the Rabbinical Alliance of America.

46. An exception to this widely held Jewish position is found in the opposition to Rabbi Nosson Slifkin. This popular Israeli Orthodox "zoo rabbi" enthusiastically supports Darwinian science in his books and public programs, while drawing from a number of traditional Jewish sources to support this view. From their stronghold in Mea Shearim in Jerusalem, some ultra-Orthodox rabbis have condemned Slifkin because they reject Darwin and think the world is 6,000 years old. Jennie Rothenberg argues that the case has more to do with a power struggle within ultra-Orthodox Judaism than with Jewish views of evolution. Rothenberg, "The Heresy of Nosson Slifkin," *Moment* (October 2005).

47. The publication of three books marks the beginning of ID. Percival Davis and Dean H. Kenyon, *Of Pandas and People* (Dallas: Haughton, 1989), a high school textbook; Philip Johnson, *Darwin on Trial* (Washington, D.C.: Regnery Gateway, 1991); and Michael J. Behe, *Darwin's Black Box* (New York: Free Press, 1996).

48. Paraphrase of "Top Questions and Answers about Intelligent Design Theory" by the Discovery Institute staff, http://www.discovery.org/script.

49. Philip Kitcher, "Born-Again Creationism," in Robert T. Pennock, ed., *Intelligent Design Creationism and Its Critics* (Cambridge: MIT Press, 2001).

50. Michael Ruse, *The Evolution-Creation Struggle* (Cambridge: Harvard University Press, 2005), 255.

51. Kitcher in "Born-Again Creationism."

52. "Top Questions and Answers about Intelligent Design Theory."

53. Behe, *Darwin's Black Box*, 5.

54. The Discovery Institute has no faith statement as creationist organizations do and includes almost no discussion of Genesis. An exception to this is Paul Nelson, a Fellow at the institute who is sympathetic to Young Earth Creationism and discusses Genesis. See Paul Nelson and John Mark Reynolds, "Young Earth

Creationism," in J. P. Moreland and J. M. Reynolds, eds., *Three Views on Creation and Evolution* (Grand Rapids: Zondervan, 1999). Also, ID supporter Alvin Plantinga is not a literalist but thinks Genesis important (Plantinga, "When Faith and Reason Clash: Evolution and the Bible," in Pennock, *Intelligest Design Creationism*).

55. Ted Peters and Martinez Hewlett also argue that ID is not creationism in *Evolution from Creationism to New Creation* (Nashville: Abingdon, 2003), 103. Further, since Genesis is not central to ID discussions, it is opposed by two prominent creationists, Henry Morris and Hugh Ross.

EPILOGUE

1. Much of the change began with the Immigration Act of 1965, and today immigrants are coming with their religions to America from more geographically diverse backgrounds than before. Diana L. Eck and her Pluralism Project at Harvard University are documenting this change and find (as of August 2006) 2150 centers representing Buddhism, 1,583 Islam, 714 Hinduism, 244 Sikhism, and others. Their website (http://pluralism.org) documents the rapid change.

2. Harold Bloom, *The American Religion: The Emergence of the Post-Christian Nation* (New York: Simon & Schuster, 1992), 229.

3. Langdon Gilkey, *Creationism on Trial: Evolution and God at Little Rock* (Charlottesville: University Press of Virginia, 1998), 198. Originally published in 1985.

4. Astronauts William Anders, Jim Lovell, and Frank Borman each read a section. They were named "Men of the Year" by *Time* on January 3, 1969, in a story that told of the reading. The version used was the King James, which for many today gives an out-of-date interpretation of some of the verses.

5. Two that I have visited recently are the American Museum of Natural History with its adjacent Rose Center for Earth and Space (a national treasure, in Manhattan) and the New Mexico Museum of Natural History (an excellent regional model). The need to put "natural" in the names of these institutions shows the anthro-

pocentrism of human outlooks; history, as feminists say, is sadly *his*-story.

APPENDIX A

1. The RSV and NRSV translators attempted to avoid a Christian bias in translating the Hebrew text. For example, both translate the Hebrew word *alma* in Isaiah 7:14 "young woman." The NIV has "a virgin will conceive," as does the old KJ—translation popular among evangelicals because it mirrors the "a virgin shall conceive" of Matthew 1:23. Another reason evangelicals do not like the NRSV is because it is copyrighted by the National Council of the Churches of Christ, with profits from sales going to the NCCC. This ecumenical organization is considered "liberal" by most evangelicals, who do not wish to give it support.

2. *Christianity Today* 41 (October 27, 1997) carried articles by Wayne Gruden (against inclusive language) and Grant Osborne (for). In several self-described "Bible bookstores" I have visited, the NRSV is not on their shelves, although some have the TNIV. In these stores the NIV is clearly the most popular.

3. "On Today's New International Version," available on the SBC website.

4. William Keeler, "The NRSV, the Revised NAB and the Liturgy," *Origins* 24, no. 22 (November 10, 1994). Richard J. Clifford, "The Rocky Road to a New Lectionary," *America* 177, no. 4 (1997).

5. Keeler, "The NRSV."

6. Per Ola and Emily D'Aulaire, "Inscribing the Word," *Smithsonian* 31, no. 9 (December 2000). The chief calligrapher is Donald Jackson of Wales, calligrapher to the Queen. The monks wanted a Bible that is "contemporary, ecumenical, multicultural, and prophetic."

APPENDIX B

1. Judge Jones, who was appointed by ID supporter President George W. Bush, is a member of a congregation of the Evangelical Lutheran Church in America. Mark A. Staples, "'Not Science': Judge John E. Jones," *The Lutheran* 19, no. 10 (October 2006).

INDEX

'adam from 'adama, 56
'adam, 11, 35, 56
Adam and Eve, 12, 33, 47, 84
American Indians, 55, 103–4
androgyny, 10–11, 123n20
anthropomorphism, 1, 8–9,
    42
apocalypse, 72
astronauts reading creation
    story, 106
Augustine, 12–13, 86

Baals and Ashteroth.
    See sexuality of the gods
Bal Talshcit, 58
Bartholomew, Ecumenical
    Patriarch, 51, 62
Behe, Michael, 97
Benedict XVI, 92
Berry, Thomas, 71, 136n54
Bible colleges, 82, 138n20

biblical authority, 18–20,
    125n36. See also
    fundamentalism
biblical criticism, 15–18, 104
    origins of, 16
    historical criticism, 16
    other types, 16–17
    feminist views, 17, 124n31
    mainline churches, 21–22
    Presbyterian Church, 91
    Roman Catholic Church, 22
    Judaism, 23, 127n44
Bloom, Harold, 36–37, 104
body of God (universe as),
    45, 64
Book of J, The, 36–37
Brueggemann, Walter, 57
Bryan College, 75–76
Bryan, William Jennings, 75,
    86, 115–16
Bush, George W., 54